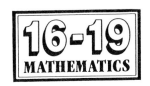

Matrices

Unit guide

The School Mathematics Project

The right of the
University of Cambridge
to print and sell
all manner of books
was granted by
Henry VIII in 1534.
The University has printed
and published continuously
since 1584.

Cambridge University Press

Cambridge   New York   Port Chester   Melbourne   Sydney

Main authors	Simon Baxter
	Stan Dolan
	Doug French
	Andy Hall
	Barrie Hunt
	Lorna Lyons
Team leader	Barrie Hunt
Project director	Stan Dolan

The authors would like to give special thanks to Ann White for her help in preparing this book for publication.

Illustrations by Andy Hall

Published by the Press Syndicate of the University of Cambridge
The Pitt Building, Trumpington Street, Cambridge CB2 1RP
40 West 20th Street, New York, NY 10011-4211, USA
10 Stamford Road, Oakleigh, Melbourne 3166, Australia

© Cambridge University Press 1991

First published 1991

Produced by Laserwords and 16-19 Mathematics, Southampton

Printed in Great Britain by Scotprint Ltd., Musselburgh.

ISBN 0 521 42662 6

Contents

Introduction to the unit
(for the teacher)

This unit has been designed so that it can be started early in an advanced level course. The entire unit requires few mathematical prerequisites beyond GCSE and, for students who have already met matrices, a selective omission of parts of the first chapter may be appropriate.

Some elementary ideas of probability are needed for the application to Stochastic matrices but this can easily be made self-contained. Students who have previously studied vectors should be encouraged to tie their knowledge of vectors into the work of this unit. For example, in Chapter 3, an infinite solution set of the form

$$x = -1 + \lambda, \ y = -1 + \lambda, \ z = \lambda$$

can be connected with the vector equation of the line of solutions:

$$\begin{bmatrix} x \\ y \\ z \end{bmatrix} = \begin{bmatrix} -1 \\ -1 \\ 0 \end{bmatrix} + \lambda \begin{bmatrix} 1 \\ 1 \\ 1 \end{bmatrix}.$$

In later chapters, a basic knowledge of the vector equations of lines and planes would be of considerable advantage. The concepts covered in these chapters require a much higher level of mathematical maturity than those covered in the first three chapters.

Chapter 1

The concept of a matrix as an array of data is used to develop natural definitions for the matrix operations of addition and multiplication. Properties of matrix arithmetic are discussed and compared with those of real number arithmetic. Practical applications are described and transition matrices introduced.

Chapter 2

A major application of matrices is in the representation of geometric transformations. The matrices of simple transformations are developed and the role of base vectors in determining the matrices of more complex transformations is described. Matrix multiplication is used to find the combination of two transformations and the significance of the inverse matrix is also explored.

Chapter 3

This chapter covers the solution of 2 x 2 and 3 x 3 simultaneous equations. Problems of existence and uniqueness are considered from a geometric viewpoint and the concept of a 'crushing transformation' is introduced.

Chapter 4

The problem of identifying the transformation represented by any 2 x 2 matrix is tackled through investigation of invariant points and lines. This leads to the important technique of finding eigenvalues and eigenvectors. The strength of this technique is demonstrated by applying it to finding powers of a matrix and to transition matrices. The surprising result of the Cayley-Hamilton theorem rounds off the chapter.

Chapter 5

Here, practical ways of solving large sets of simultaneous equations are considered. The techniques of Gaussian elimination, LU decomposition and Gauss Seidel iteration are described and compared. Problems of implementation are discussed and ill conditioned equations considered.

Students are encouraged to investigate numerical methods for solving simultaneous equations. Designing algorithms is a challenging exercise for those who enjoy programming. For those who find this less interesting, short and simple programs are listed at the end of this unit guide.

Chapter 6

In this chapter, the work of Chapter 3 is generalised to sets of m x n equations. The idea of a general solution comprising a kernel and particular solution is introduced and methods of determining the kernel are considered. Row operations are used to reduce a matrix to a canonical form from which the general solution to a matrix equation can be readily found.

Tasksheets

1   *Introduction to matrices*

1.3   Properties of matrix arithmetic

> **(a)** Find two matrices which cannot be added together.
>
> **(b)** Can you find a scalar and a matrix which cannot be multiplied together?
>
> **(c)** Can you find two matrices which cannot be multiplied together?
>
> **(d)** Describe the conditions under which each of the types of calculation described above can be carried out.

(a) Any pair which are not of the same order.

For example, $\begin{bmatrix} 1 & 2 \\ 3 & 4 \end{bmatrix} + \begin{bmatrix} 5 \\ 6 \end{bmatrix}$

(b) No, scalar multiplication can always be performed.

(c) Any pair where the number of columns of the first matrix is not the same as the number of rows of the second.

For example, $\begin{bmatrix} 1 & 2 \\ 3 & 4 \end{bmatrix} \begin{bmatrix} 5 & 6 \end{bmatrix}$

(d) It is only possible to **add** an $m \times n$ matrix to another $m \times n$ matrix and to **multiply** an $m \times n$ matrix by an $n \times p$ matrix.

Matrix arithmetic

1. (a) (i) $\begin{bmatrix} 12 & 20 & 18 \\ 8 & 11 & 8 \end{bmatrix}$ (ii) $\begin{bmatrix} 29 & 32 & 33 \\ 30 & 27 & 19 \end{bmatrix}$

    (b) Till 3 – Till 2 = $\begin{bmatrix} 14 & 4 & 8 \\ 17 & 12 & 5 \end{bmatrix}$

2. (a) $\begin{bmatrix} 8 & 6 \\ 3 & 8 \\ 9 & 9 \end{bmatrix}$ (b) $\begin{bmatrix} 5 & 2 \\ 6 & 3 \end{bmatrix}$ (c) $\begin{bmatrix} a_{11} + b_{11} & a_{12} + b_{12} & a_{13} + b_{13} \\ a_{21} + b_{21} & a_{22} + b_{22} & a_{23} + b_{23} \end{bmatrix}$

3. $12 \times \begin{bmatrix} 9 & 12 & 11 \\ 3 & 7 & 2 \end{bmatrix} = \begin{bmatrix} 108 & 144 & 132 \\ 36 & 84 & 24 \end{bmatrix}$

4. (a) $\begin{bmatrix} 15 & 10 & 25 \\ 20 & 5 & 15 \end{bmatrix}$ (b) $\begin{bmatrix} 2 & 1.5 \\ 0.5 & 1 \end{bmatrix}$ (c) $\begin{bmatrix} ka_{11} & ka_{12} & ka_{13} \\ ka_{21} & ka_{22} & ka_{23} \end{bmatrix}$

5. (a) The total number of component A is $2 \times 7 + 1 \times 12 + 3 \times 3 = 35$ i.e. each element of row 1 is multiplied by the number of each type of radio. Calculating the totals for components B and C gives the result

$$\begin{bmatrix} 2 & 1 & 3 \\ 4 & 2 & 1 \\ 2 & 3 & 3 \end{bmatrix} \begin{bmatrix} 7 \\ 12 \\ 3 \end{bmatrix} = \begin{bmatrix} 2 \times 7 + 1 \times 12 + 3 \times 3 \\ 4 \times 7 + 2 \times 12 + 1 \times 3 \\ 2 \times 7 + 3 \times 12 + 3 \times 3 \end{bmatrix} = \begin{bmatrix} 35 \\ 55 \\ 59 \end{bmatrix}$$

Thus the multiplication of the two matrices is performed by multiplying each row in turn by the single column matrix.

    (b) $\begin{bmatrix} 90 & 48 & 73 \end{bmatrix} \begin{bmatrix} 2 & 1 & 3 \\ 4 & 2 & 1 \\ 2 & 3 & 3 \end{bmatrix} = \begin{bmatrix} 180 & 90 & 270 \\ + & + & + \\ 192 & 96 & 48 \\ + & + & + \\ 146 & 219 & 219 \end{bmatrix} = \begin{bmatrix} 518 & 405 & 537 \end{bmatrix}$

6. (a) $\begin{bmatrix} 3 & 4 \\ 2 & 1 \\ 6 & 7 \\ 9 & 2 \end{bmatrix} \begin{bmatrix} 5 \\ 1 \end{bmatrix} = \begin{bmatrix} 15 + 4 \\ 10 + 1 \\ 30 + 7 \\ 45 + 2 \end{bmatrix} = \begin{bmatrix} 19 \\ 11 \\ 37 \\ 47 \end{bmatrix}$

    (b) $\begin{bmatrix} 3 & 7 & 9 & 1 \end{bmatrix} \begin{bmatrix} 4 \\ 7 \\ 9 \\ 3 \end{bmatrix} = \begin{bmatrix} 12 + 49 + 91 + 3 \end{bmatrix} = \begin{bmatrix} 145 \end{bmatrix}$

(continued)

7. (a) (i)   In one second, the amount of water arriving at α is

$$\tfrac{1}{2} \times \text{(water from } A \text{)} + \tfrac{1}{3} \times \text{(water from } B \text{)}$$

$$= \tfrac{1}{2} \times 16 + \tfrac{1}{3} \times 9 = 8 + 3 = 11 \text{ litres}$$

Similarly, the amount arriving at β per second is

$$\tfrac{1}{2} \times 16 + \tfrac{2}{3} \times 9 = 8 + 6 = 14 \text{ litres}$$

(ii)
$$\begin{bmatrix} \tfrac{1}{2} & \tfrac{1}{3} \\ \tfrac{1}{2} & \tfrac{2}{3} \end{bmatrix} \begin{bmatrix} 16 \\ 9 \end{bmatrix} = \begin{bmatrix} 11 \\ 14 \end{bmatrix}$$

The matrix $\begin{bmatrix} 16 \\ 9 \end{bmatrix}$ represents the rates of flow from A and B, whilst the matrix $\begin{bmatrix} 11 \\ 14 \end{bmatrix}$ represents the rates of flow into α and β.

(iii) If the rates are A and B litres per second respectively

$$\tfrac{1}{2} A + \tfrac{1}{3} B = 20$$

$$\tfrac{1}{2} A + \tfrac{2}{3} B = 25$$

$$\Rightarrow B = 15, \ A = 30$$

(b) (i)   In 1 second, the proportion of water flowing from A to a

$$= \text{(proportion of water from } A \text{ to } \alpha \text{ to } a \text{)} +$$
$$\text{(proportion of water from } A \text{ to } \beta \text{ to } a \text{)}$$

$$= \tfrac{1}{2} \times \tfrac{1}{4} + \tfrac{1}{2} \times \tfrac{4}{5} = \tfrac{1}{8} + \tfrac{2}{5} = \tfrac{21}{40}$$

Similarly, the proportion flowing from A to b

is $\tfrac{1}{2} \times \tfrac{3}{4} + \tfrac{1}{2} \times \tfrac{1}{5} = \tfrac{3}{8} + \tfrac{1}{10} = \tfrac{19}{40}$

The proportion flowing from B to a is $\tfrac{1}{3} \times \tfrac{1}{4} + \tfrac{2}{3} \times \tfrac{4}{5} = \tfrac{1}{12} + \tfrac{8}{15} = \tfrac{37}{60}$

and from B to b is $\tfrac{1}{3} \times \tfrac{3}{4} + \tfrac{2}{3} \times \tfrac{1}{5} = \tfrac{1}{4} + \tfrac{2}{15} = \tfrac{23}{60}$

(ii)
$$\begin{bmatrix} \tfrac{21}{40} & \tfrac{37}{60} \\ \tfrac{19}{40} & \tfrac{23}{60} \end{bmatrix}$$

(continued)

(iii) If $\begin{bmatrix} r \\ s \end{bmatrix}$ is the flow arriving/leaving stations α, β and $\begin{bmatrix} t \\ u \end{bmatrix}$ is the flow arriving at a, b each second

$$\begin{bmatrix} r \\ s \end{bmatrix} = \begin{bmatrix} \frac{1}{2} & \frac{1}{3} \\ \frac{1}{2} & \frac{2}{3} \end{bmatrix} \begin{bmatrix} p \\ q \end{bmatrix}$$

$$\begin{bmatrix} t \\ u \end{bmatrix} = \begin{bmatrix} \frac{1}{4} & \frac{4}{5} \\ \frac{3}{4} & \frac{1}{5} \end{bmatrix} \begin{bmatrix} r \\ s \end{bmatrix} = \begin{bmatrix} \frac{1}{4} & \frac{4}{5} \\ \frac{3}{4} & \frac{1}{5} \end{bmatrix} \begin{bmatrix} \frac{1}{2} & \frac{1}{3} \\ \frac{1}{2} & \frac{2}{3} \end{bmatrix} \begin{bmatrix} p \\ q \end{bmatrix}$$

(iv) $\begin{bmatrix} \frac{1}{4} & \frac{4}{5} \\ \frac{3}{4} & \frac{1}{5} \end{bmatrix} \begin{bmatrix} \frac{1}{2} & \frac{1}{3} \\ \frac{1}{2} & \frac{2}{3} \end{bmatrix} = \begin{bmatrix} \frac{1}{4}\times\frac{1}{2} + \frac{4}{5}\times\frac{1}{2} & \frac{1}{4}\times\frac{1}{3} + \frac{4}{5}\times\frac{2}{3} \\ \frac{3}{4}\times\frac{1}{2} + \frac{1}{5}\times\frac{1}{2} & \frac{3}{4}\times\frac{1}{3} + \frac{1}{5}\times\frac{2}{3} \end{bmatrix}$

$$= \begin{bmatrix} \frac{21}{40} & \frac{37}{60} \\ \frac{19}{40} & \frac{23}{60} \end{bmatrix}$$

(v) The calculations performed in (i) correspond to the row and column operations in (iv).

(vi) $\begin{bmatrix} \frac{21}{40} & \frac{37}{60} \\ \frac{19}{40} & \frac{23}{60} \end{bmatrix} \begin{bmatrix} 80 \\ 30 \end{bmatrix} = \begin{bmatrix} 42 + 18\frac{1}{2} \\ 38 + 11\frac{1}{2} \end{bmatrix} = \begin{bmatrix} 60\frac{1}{2} \\ 49\frac{1}{2} \end{bmatrix}$

8. (a) (i) $\begin{bmatrix} 4 & 2 & 8 \\ 3 & 3 & 7 \end{bmatrix} \begin{bmatrix} 1 & 4 \\ 6 & 1 \\ 5 & 9 \end{bmatrix} = \begin{bmatrix} 4\times1+2\times6+8\times5 & 4\times4+2\times1+8\times9 \\ 3\times1+3\times6+7\times5 & 3\times4+3\times1+7\times9 \end{bmatrix}$

$$= \begin{bmatrix} 56 & 90 \\ 56 & 78 \end{bmatrix}$$

(ii) $\begin{bmatrix} 18 & 22 \\ 7 & 13 \end{bmatrix}$

(iii) $\begin{bmatrix} 39 & -24 & 19 \\ 19 & 4 & 46 \\ -25 & -4 & -65 \\ 8 & -38 & 2 \end{bmatrix}$

(b) Since the first matrix has two columns and the second has three rows, it is impossible to perform the row/column multiplication. The two matrices are said to be incompatible.

1. (a) (i) $(73 + 996) + 4 = 73 + (996 + 4)$

    (ii) $(2 \times 3) \times 5 = 2 \times (3 \times 5)$

    (b) (i)   When three numbers are added it makes no difference whether the first pair or the second pair of numbers is added first.

    (ii)   When three numbers are multiplied it makes no difference whether the first pair or the second pair of numbers is multiplied first.

    (iii) The order of addition is immaterial.

    (iv) The order of multiplication is immaterial.

    (v)   Adding zero leaves a number unchanged.

    (vi) Multiplication by one leaves a number unchanged.

2. (i) (a) Matrix addition is associative. For example:

$$\left\{ \begin{bmatrix} 3 & 4 \\ 2 & 1 \end{bmatrix} + \begin{bmatrix} 5 & 1 \\ 3 & 4 \end{bmatrix} \right\} + \begin{bmatrix} 1 & -4 \\ 6 & 0 \end{bmatrix} = \begin{bmatrix} 8 & 5 \\ 5 & 5 \end{bmatrix} + \begin{bmatrix} 1 & -4 \\ 6 & 0 \end{bmatrix} = \begin{bmatrix} 9 & 1 \\ 11 & 5 \end{bmatrix}$$

$$\begin{bmatrix} 3 & 4 \\ 2 & 1 \end{bmatrix} + \left\{ \begin{bmatrix} 5 & 1 \\ 3 & 4 \end{bmatrix} + \begin{bmatrix} 1 & -4 \\ 6 & 0 \end{bmatrix} \right\} = \begin{bmatrix} 3 & 4 \\ 2 & 1 \end{bmatrix} + \begin{bmatrix} 6 & -3 \\ 9 & 4 \end{bmatrix} = \begin{bmatrix} 9 & 1 \\ 11 & 5 \end{bmatrix}$$

(b) $(\mathbf{A} + \mathbf{B}) + \mathbf{C} = \left\{ \begin{bmatrix} a_{11} & a_{12} \\ a_{21} & a_{22} \end{bmatrix} + \begin{bmatrix} b_{11} & b_{12} \\ b_{21} & b_{22} \end{bmatrix} \right\} + \begin{bmatrix} c_{11} & c_{12} \\ c_{21} & c_{22} \end{bmatrix}$

$= \begin{bmatrix} a_{11}+b_{11} & a_{12}+b_{12} \\ a_{21}+b_{21} & a_{22}+b_{22} \end{bmatrix} + \begin{bmatrix} c_{11} & c_{12} \\ c_{21} & c_{22} \end{bmatrix} = \begin{bmatrix} a_{11}+b_{11}+c_{11} & a_{12}+b_{12}+c_{12} \\ a_{21}+b_{21}+c_{21} & a_{22}+b_{22}+c_{22} \end{bmatrix}$

The same answer is obtained for $\mathbf{A} + (\mathbf{B} + \mathbf{C})$, since addition is associative on the real numbers.

(continued)

(iii) (a) Matrix addition is commutative.

(b) $\mathbf{A+B} = \begin{bmatrix} a_{11} & a_{12} \\ a_{21} & a_{22} \end{bmatrix} + \begin{bmatrix} b_{11} & b_{12} \\ b_{21} & b_{22} \end{bmatrix}$

$= \begin{bmatrix} a_{11} + b_{11} & a_{12} + b_{12} \\ a_{21} + b_{21} & a_{22} + b_{22} \end{bmatrix} = \begin{bmatrix} b_{11} + a_{11} & b_{12} + a_{12} \\ b_{21} + a_{21} & b_{22} + a_{22} \end{bmatrix}$

$= \begin{bmatrix} b_{11} & b_{12} \\ b_{21} & b_{22} \end{bmatrix} + \begin{bmatrix} a_{11} & a_{12} \\ a_{21} & a_{22} \end{bmatrix}$

$= \mathbf{B} + \mathbf{A}$

(iv) (a) Matrix multiplication is not commutative.

(b) One counterexample is

$\mathbf{AB} = \begin{bmatrix} 2 & 1 \\ 0 & 3 \end{bmatrix} \begin{bmatrix} 1 & 2 \\ 4 & 0 \end{bmatrix} = \begin{bmatrix} 6 & 4 \\ 12 & 0 \end{bmatrix}$

$\mathbf{BA} = \begin{bmatrix} 1 & 2 \\ 4 & 0 \end{bmatrix} \begin{bmatrix} 2 & 1 \\ 0 & 3 \end{bmatrix} = \begin{bmatrix} 2 & 7 \\ 8 & 4 \end{bmatrix} \neq \mathbf{AB}$

3. The result holds for any set of 3 matrices $\mathbf{A}, \mathbf{B}, \mathbf{C}$. For example,

$(\mathbf{AB})\mathbf{C} = \left\{ \begin{bmatrix} 1 & 2 \\ 3 & 4 \end{bmatrix} \begin{bmatrix} 2 & -1 \\ 1 & 3 \end{bmatrix} \right\} \begin{bmatrix} 4 & 1 \\ -2 & 0 \end{bmatrix} = \begin{bmatrix} 4 & 5 \\ 10 & 9 \end{bmatrix} \begin{bmatrix} 4 & 1 \\ -2 & 0 \end{bmatrix} = \begin{bmatrix} 6 & 4 \\ 22 & 10 \end{bmatrix}$

$\mathbf{A}(\mathbf{BC}) = \begin{bmatrix} 1 & 2 \\ 3 & 4 \end{bmatrix} \left\{ \begin{bmatrix} 2 & -1 \\ 1 & 3 \end{bmatrix} \begin{bmatrix} 4 & 1 \\ -2 & 0 \end{bmatrix} \right\} = \begin{bmatrix} 1 & 2 \\ 3 & 4 \end{bmatrix} \begin{bmatrix} 10 & 2 \\ -2 & 1 \end{bmatrix} = \begin{bmatrix} 6 & 4 \\ 22 & 10 \end{bmatrix} = (\mathbf{AB})\mathbf{C}$

4. $\mathbf{O} = \begin{bmatrix} 0 & 0 \\ 0 & 0 \end{bmatrix}$ since $\mathbf{O} + \mathbf{A} = \mathbf{A}$ for any matrix $\mathbf{A}$

$\mathbf{I} = \begin{bmatrix} 1 & 0 \\ 0 & 1 \end{bmatrix}$ since $\mathbf{IA} = \mathbf{A}$ for any matrix $\mathbf{A}$

5. (a) No, real number addition is closed.

(b) Yes, the product of two real numbers is real.

(c) No, for example, $4 - 7 = -3$ which is not a positive integer.

(d) Yes, the sum of two 2 x 2 matrices is a 2 x 2 matrix.

(e) Yes, the product of two 2 x 2 matrices is a 2 x 2 matrix.

(continued)

6.   (a) For example, $\begin{bmatrix} 1 & 0 \\ 2 & 1 \end{bmatrix}\begin{bmatrix} 1 & 0 \\ 3 & 1 \end{bmatrix} = \begin{bmatrix} 1 & 0 \\ 5 & 1 \end{bmatrix}$ which belongs to S.

      (b) $\begin{bmatrix} 1 & 0 \\ a & 1 \end{bmatrix}\begin{bmatrix} 1 & 0 \\ b & 1 \end{bmatrix} = \begin{bmatrix} 1 & 0 \\ a+b & 1 \end{bmatrix} \in S$, so the result is true for all $A, B \in S$.

      (c) No, for example, $\begin{bmatrix} 2 & 0 \\ 1 & 2 \end{bmatrix}\begin{bmatrix} 2 & 0 \\ 2 & 2 \end{bmatrix} = \begin{bmatrix} 4 & 0 \\ 6 & 4 \end{bmatrix}$ which is not of the right form.

7.   (a) For example $\mathbf{A} = \begin{bmatrix} 1 & 0 & 0 \\ 0 & 2 & 0 \\ 0 & 0 & 3 \end{bmatrix}$ $\mathbf{B} = \begin{bmatrix} -4 & 0 & 0 \\ 0 & 3 & 0 \\ 0 & 0 & 5 \end{bmatrix}$

$$\mathbf{AB} = \begin{bmatrix} 1 & 0 & 0 \\ 0 & 2 & 0 \\ 0 & 0 & 3 \end{bmatrix}\begin{bmatrix} -4 & 0 & 0 \\ 0 & 3 & 0 \\ 0 & 0 & 5 \end{bmatrix} = \begin{bmatrix} -4 & 0 & 0 \\ 0 & 6 & 0 \\ 0 & 0 & 15 \end{bmatrix}$$

$$\mathbf{BA} = \begin{bmatrix} -4 & 0 & 0 \\ 0 & 3 & 0 \\ 0 & 0 & 5 \end{bmatrix}\begin{bmatrix} 1 & 0 & 0 \\ 0 & 2 & 0 \\ 0 & 0 & 3 \end{bmatrix} = \begin{bmatrix} -4 & 0 & 0 \\ 0 & 6 & 0 \\ 0 & 0 & 15 \end{bmatrix}$$

(b)   The set is closed since, for general $\mathbf{A}, \mathbf{B}$

$$\mathbf{AB} = \begin{bmatrix} a_{11} & 0 & 0 \\ 0 & a_{22} & 0 \\ 0 & 0 & a_{33} \end{bmatrix}\begin{bmatrix} b_{11} & 0 & 0 \\ 0 & b_{22} & 0 \\ 0 & 0 & b_{33} \end{bmatrix}$$

$$= \begin{bmatrix} a_{11}b_{11} & 0 & 0 \\ 0 & a_{22}b_{22} & 0 \\ 0 & 0 & a_{33}b_{33} \end{bmatrix}, \text{ which is of the same form.}$$

      Thus matrix multiplication is closed on this set.

Leslie matrices

1.   Not greatly, though women tend to live longer than men and will therefore have a greater representation in the older age groups.

2.   (a)   4.6 million.

       (b)   The total number of births and the number of deaths in each age group.

3.   (a)   The population matrix structure does not allow for an age group beyond $60 - 74$ so the model must assume that no one survives.

       (b)   (i)   The number in the age group $30 - 44$

                 $=$ (number in the age group $15 - 29$) x (probability of survival)

                 $=$ 6.6 x 0.99 047 $=$ 6.537 million.

           (ii)   The number in the age group $0 - 14$

                 $=$ number born to mothers aged $0 - 14$ + number born to mothers aged $15 - 29$ + number born to mothers aged $30 - 44$

                 $=$ 5.2 x 0.05885 + 6.6 x 1.09798 + 5.8 x 0.13523

                 $=$ 8.337 million.

4.   (a)   The population matrix in 15 years time is $\mathbf{Lp_0}$.

           In 30 years it will be $\mathbf{L(Lp_0)} = \mathbf{L^2 p_0}$ and in 45 years $\mathbf{L(L^2 p_0)} = \mathbf{L^3 p_0}$.

           It is not possible to calculate the age structure in 100 years time from this data. However, the population matrix will be $\mathbf{L^6 p_0}$ in 90 years and $\mathbf{L^7 p_0}$ in 105 years.

       (b)   This assumes that survival and fertility rates remain constant. Both these assumptions are very unlikely!

5.   (a) $\mathbf{L} = \begin{bmatrix} 1.12 & 0.5 & 0.1 \\ 0.9 & 0 & 0 \\ 0 & 0.7 & 0 \end{bmatrix}$

       (b) $\mathbf{L^2} \begin{bmatrix} 80 \\ 50 \\ 40 \end{bmatrix} = \mathbf{L} \begin{bmatrix} 118.6 \\ 72 \\ 35 \end{bmatrix} = \begin{bmatrix} 172.3 \\ 106.7 \\ 50.4 \end{bmatrix}$

(continued)

6.   Suppose the intial population matrix is $\mathbf{p}_0 = \begin{bmatrix} 100 \\ 100 \\ 100 \\ 100 \\ 100 \\ 100 \\ 100 \end{bmatrix}$

$$\mathbf{p}_1 = \begin{bmatrix} 78 \\ 66 \\ 93 \\ 93 \\ 93 \\ 93.5 \\ 187 \end{bmatrix}, \quad \mathbf{p}_2 = \begin{bmatrix} 112.2 \\ 51.5 \\ 61.4 \\ 86.5 \\ 86.5 \\ 87.0 \\ 262.3 \end{bmatrix}, \quad \mathbf{p}_3 = \begin{bmatrix} 141.4 \\ 74.1 \\ 47.9 \\ 57.1 \\ 80.4 \\ 80.9 \\ 326.6 \end{bmatrix}$$

Total
population   703.5   747.4   808.4

It is clear that the population is growing in total, though the obvious longer term question is whether sufficient pups will survive to reach the breeding ages of 4, 5 and 6 years.

Tutorial sheet

1. (a) (i) 3 x 2 multiplied by 2 x 4 gives a 3 x 4 matrix.
        (ii) 2 x 3
        (iii) 3 x 3
        (iv) 3 x 3

    (b) $\mathbf{A}(\mathbf{BC}) = (\mathbf{AB})\mathbf{C} = \begin{bmatrix} 307 & 194 & 292 \\ 703 & 444 & 683 \\ 1170 & 742 & 955 \end{bmatrix}$

    The associative law $\mathbf{A}(\mathbf{BC}) = (\mathbf{AB})\mathbf{C}$ can be shown to apply to non-square matrices.

2. Let $\mathbf{A} = \begin{bmatrix} a_{11} & a_{12} \\ a_{21} & a_{22} \end{bmatrix}$ $\mathbf{B} = \begin{bmatrix} b_{11} & b_{12} \\ b_{21} & b_{22} \end{bmatrix}$ $\mathbf{C} = \begin{bmatrix} c_{11} & c_{12} \\ c_{21} & c_{22} \end{bmatrix}$

    $\mathbf{A}(\mathbf{B} + \mathbf{C}) = \begin{bmatrix} a_{11} & a_{12} \\ a_{21} & a_{22} \end{bmatrix}\begin{bmatrix} b_{11} + c_{11} & b_{12} + c_{12} \\ b_{21} + c_{21} & b_{22} + c_{22} \end{bmatrix}$

    $= \begin{bmatrix} a_{11}(b_{11}+c_{11}) + a_{12}(b_{21}+c_{21}) & a_{11}(b_{12}+c_{12}) + a_{12}(b_{22}+c_{22}) \\ a_{21}(b_{11}+c_{11}) + a_{22}(b_{21}+c_{21}) & a_{21}(b_{12}+c_{12}) + a_{22}(b_{22}+c_{22}) \end{bmatrix}$

    $\mathbf{AB} + \mathbf{AC} = \begin{bmatrix} a_{11}b_{11} + a_{12}b_{21} & a_{11}b_{12} + a_{12}b_{22} \\ a_{21}b_{11} + a_{22}b_{21} & a_{21}b_{12} + a_{22}b_{22} \end{bmatrix} + \begin{bmatrix} a_{11}c_{11} + a_{12}c_{21} & a_{11}c_{12} + a_{12}c_{22} \\ a_{21}c_{11} + a_{22}c_{21} & a_{21}c_{12} + a_{22}c_{22} \end{bmatrix}$

    $= \mathbf{A}(\mathbf{B} + \mathbf{C})$

3. (a) $(a + b)^2 = (a + b)(a + b)$

    $= a(a + b) + b(a + b)$ distributive law

    $= (a^2 + ab) + (ba + b^2)$ distributive law

    $= a^2 + ab + ba + b^2$ associative law for addition

    $= a^2 + 2ab + b^2$ commutative law for multiplication

    $= a^2 + b^2 + 2ab$ commutative law for addition

    (b) (ii) The commutative law does not hold for multiplication of matrices
        i.e. $\mathbf{AB} \neq \mathbf{BA}$.

    (iii) The proof in (a) is valid until the commutative law is applied. Therefore,
        $(\mathbf{A} + \mathbf{B})^2 = \mathbf{A}^2 + \mathbf{AB} + \mathbf{BA} + \mathbf{B}^2$.

(continued)

4. (a) $$\begin{bmatrix} 5 & 3 & 2 & 1 & 2 \\ 3 & 2 & 1 & 3 & 2 \\ 1 & 0 & 0 & 1 & 1 \\ 2 & 2 & 0 & 6 & 3 \\ 3 & 1 & 1 & 3 & 3 \end{bmatrix}$$

    (b) $\mathbf{R}^2$ is the same matrix as in (a).

    (c) $\mathbf{R}^3$ will represent the total number of three-step journeys between each pair of stops.

5. (a) The probability is zero.

    (b) $\frac{15}{22}$

    (c)
    $$\mathbf{T} = \begin{array}{c} \\ W \\ E \end{array} \begin{array}{cc} W & E \\ \begin{bmatrix} 0 & \frac{7}{22} \\ 1 & \frac{15}{22} \end{bmatrix} \end{array}$$

    (d) For 1991 $\begin{bmatrix} 0 & \frac{7}{22} \\ 1 & \frac{15}{22} \end{bmatrix} \begin{bmatrix} 1 \\ 0 \end{bmatrix} = \begin{bmatrix} 0 \\ 1 \end{bmatrix}$ Wales are certain to win (which in fact did not happen!)

    for 1992 $\begin{bmatrix} 0 & \frac{7}{22} \\ 1 & \frac{15}{22} \end{bmatrix} \begin{bmatrix} 0 \\ 1 \end{bmatrix} = \begin{bmatrix} \frac{7}{22} \\ \frac{15}{22} \end{bmatrix}$

    for 1993 $\begin{bmatrix} 0 & \frac{7}{22} \\ 1 & \frac{15}{22} \end{bmatrix} \begin{bmatrix} \frac{7}{22} \\ \frac{15}{22} \end{bmatrix} = \begin{bmatrix} 0.22 \\ 0.78 \end{bmatrix}$

    P (England win) = 0.22, P (Wales win) = 0.78.

6. (a) $\begin{bmatrix} -1 & 0 \\ 0 & -1 \end{bmatrix}$ and $\begin{bmatrix} \frac{1}{\sqrt{2}} & \frac{1}{\sqrt{2}} \\ \frac{1}{\sqrt{2}} & -\frac{1}{\sqrt{2}} \end{bmatrix}$ are two of the many possibilities.

    (b) There are many possibilities, for example $\begin{bmatrix} 2 & -2 \\ 2 & -2 \end{bmatrix}$

2 *Matrices and transformations*

2.2 Describing transformations

(a)

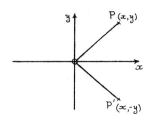

$$\begin{bmatrix} 1 & 0 \\ 0 & -1 \end{bmatrix} \begin{bmatrix} x \\ y \end{bmatrix} = \begin{bmatrix} x \\ -y \end{bmatrix}$$

so the matrix is $\begin{bmatrix} 1 & 0 \\ 0 & -1 \end{bmatrix}$

(b)

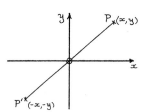

$$\begin{bmatrix} x \\ y \end{bmatrix} \rightarrow \begin{bmatrix} -x \\ -y \end{bmatrix}$$

$$\begin{bmatrix} -1 & 0 \\ 0 & -1 \end{bmatrix}$$

(c)

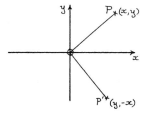

$$\begin{bmatrix} x \\ y \end{bmatrix} \rightarrow \begin{bmatrix} y \\ -x \end{bmatrix}$$

$$\begin{bmatrix} 0 & 1 \\ -1 & 0 \end{bmatrix}$$

(d)

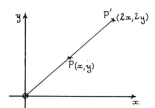

$$\begin{bmatrix} x \\ y \end{bmatrix} \rightarrow \begin{bmatrix} 2x \\ 2y \end{bmatrix}$$

$$\begin{bmatrix} 2 & 0 \\ 0 & 2 \end{bmatrix}$$

Transformations

1. The centre and the sense (clockwise or anti-clockwise).

2. It is sufficient to give the mirror line for a reflection.

3. (a) $F_1 \rightarrow F_2$, $\begin{bmatrix} -3 \\ 1 \end{bmatrix}$ (b) $F_2 \rightarrow F_3$, $\begin{bmatrix} 1 \\ -2 \end{bmatrix}$ (c) $F_3 \rightarrow F_1$, $\begin{bmatrix} 2 \\ 1 \end{bmatrix}$

$F_1 \rightarrow F_2 \rightarrow F_3 \rightarrow F_1$, returns to the starting point. The

vectors should therefore add to $\begin{bmatrix} 0 \\ 0 \end{bmatrix}$.

4. (a) Scale factor $\frac{1}{2}$. The image becomes smaller.

    (b) Half turn about the centre of the enlargement.

    (c)

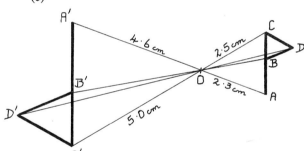

The scale factor is –2.

The -ve sign indicates that the object and image points are on opposite sides of the centre of enlargement.

5. (a) A translation through $\begin{bmatrix} 0 \\ 0 \end{bmatrix}$; (b) An enlargement of scale factor 1.

6. (a) Translation $\begin{bmatrix} 6 \\ -11 \end{bmatrix}$;

    (b) Anti-clockwise rotation of 120° about (3, –4);

    (c) Enlargement, scale factor –2, centre (0, 0);

    (d) Reflection in $y = \frac{1}{2}x$.

(continued)

7.

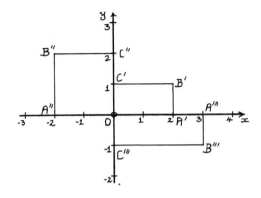

8.   (a)

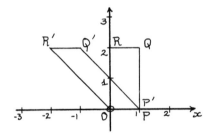

(b)

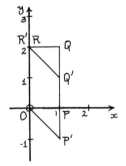

Describing transformations

1. (a) Rotation centre $(0, 0)$ angle $45°$, enlargement s.f. $\sqrt{2}$, centre $(0, 0)$. The transformations can be done in either order.

    (b) $\begin{bmatrix} 0 \\ 0 \end{bmatrix} \rightarrow \begin{bmatrix} 0 \\ 0 \end{bmatrix}$; $\begin{bmatrix} 1 \\ 0 \end{bmatrix} \rightarrow \begin{bmatrix} 1 \\ 1 \end{bmatrix}$; $\begin{bmatrix} 1 \\ 1 \end{bmatrix} \rightarrow \begin{bmatrix} 0 \\ 2 \end{bmatrix}$; $\begin{bmatrix} 0 \\ 1 \end{bmatrix} \rightarrow \begin{bmatrix} -1 \\ 1 \end{bmatrix}$

    (c) $\begin{bmatrix} 1 \\ 1 \end{bmatrix}$; $\begin{bmatrix} 0.8 \\ 1.2 \end{bmatrix}$; $\begin{bmatrix} 0.6 \\ 1.4 \end{bmatrix}$; $\begin{bmatrix} 0.4 \\ 1.6 \end{bmatrix}$; $\begin{bmatrix} 0.2 \\ 1.8 \end{bmatrix}$; $\begin{bmatrix} 0 \\ 2 \end{bmatrix}$.

    (d) $a = 1$, $b = -1$, $c = 1$, $d = 1$

    (e) $\begin{bmatrix} 1 & -1 \\ 1 & 1 \end{bmatrix}$

2. (a) All points on the x-axis are invariant
        Straight lines transform to straight lines.
        Areas are invariant.
        A point at distance y from the x-axis moves $2y$ to the right.

    (b) $\begin{bmatrix} 1 \\ 0 \end{bmatrix}$; $\begin{bmatrix} 1.4 \\ 0.2 \end{bmatrix}$; $\begin{bmatrix} 1.8 \\ 0.4 \end{bmatrix}$; $\begin{bmatrix} 2.2 \\ 0.6 \end{bmatrix}$; $\begin{bmatrix} 2.6 \\ 0.8 \end{bmatrix}$; $\begin{bmatrix} 3 \\ 1 \end{bmatrix}$.

    (c) $\begin{bmatrix} 1 & 2 \\ 0 & 1 \end{bmatrix}$

3. (a) Straight lines transform to straight lines; the origin is invariant.

    (b) Enlargement is a two-way stretch with **equal** factors.

    (c) $P\,(1, 0) \rightarrow P'\,(3, 0)$; $Q\,(1, 1) \rightarrow Q'\,(3, 2)$; $R\,(0, 1) \rightarrow R'\,(0, 2)$ and
        $S\,(-1, -1) \rightarrow S'\,(-3, -2)$

    (d) $\begin{bmatrix} 3 & 0 \\ 0 & 2 \end{bmatrix}$

4. (a) $\begin{bmatrix} 2 \\ 1 \end{bmatrix}$; $\begin{bmatrix} 1.8 \\ 1 \end{bmatrix}$; $\begin{bmatrix} 1.6 \\ 1 \end{bmatrix}$; $\begin{bmatrix} 1.4 \\ 1 \end{bmatrix}$; $\begin{bmatrix} 1.2 \\ 1 \end{bmatrix}$; $\begin{bmatrix} 1 \\ 1 \end{bmatrix}$.

    (b) $a = 2$, $b = -1$, $c = 1$, $d = 0$.

    (c) $\begin{bmatrix} 2 & -1 \\ 1 & 0 \end{bmatrix}$

1.   (a)

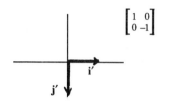

$\begin{bmatrix} 1 & 0 \\ 0 & -1 \end{bmatrix}$

     (b)

$\begin{bmatrix} 1 & 0 \\ 0 & 1 \end{bmatrix}$

   (c)

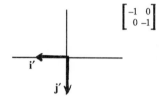

$\begin{bmatrix} -1 & 0 \\ 0 & -1 \end{bmatrix}$

     (d)

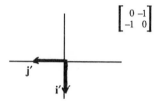

$\begin{bmatrix} 0 & -1 \\ -1 & 0 \end{bmatrix}$

   (e)

$\begin{bmatrix} 2 & 0 \\ 0 & 2 \end{bmatrix}$

     (f)

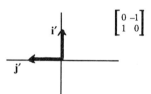

$\begin{bmatrix} 0 & -1 \\ 1 & 0 \end{bmatrix}$

   (g)

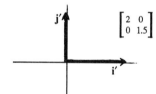

$\begin{bmatrix} 2 & 0 \\ 0 & 1.5 \end{bmatrix}$

     (h)

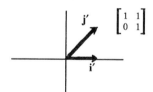

$\begin{bmatrix} 1 & 1 \\ 0 & 1 \end{bmatrix}$

2.   (a)

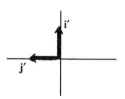

Rotation about (0, 0) of 90°

     (b)

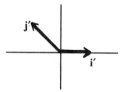

Shear, x-axis invariant

$(0, 1) \rightarrow (-1, 1)$

(continued)

2.   (c)

Enlargement scale factor $\frac{1}{2}$,
centre $(0, 0)$

       (d)

Reflection in $y = x$

       (e)

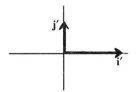

One-way stretch parallel to $0x$, scale factor 2

       (f)

Reflection in y-axis

3.   (a)

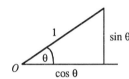 $\begin{bmatrix} 1 \\ 0 \end{bmatrix} \rightarrow \begin{bmatrix} \cos\theta \\ \sin\theta \end{bmatrix}$

       (b) $\begin{bmatrix} 0 \\ 1 \end{bmatrix} \rightarrow \begin{bmatrix} -\sin\theta \\ \cos\theta \end{bmatrix}$ (c) $\begin{bmatrix} \cos\theta & -\sin\theta \\ \sin\theta & \cos\theta \end{bmatrix}$

       (d) $R_{0°} = \begin{bmatrix} 1 & 0 \\ 0 & 1 \end{bmatrix}$; $R_{90°} = \begin{bmatrix} 0 & -1 \\ 1 & 0 \end{bmatrix}$; $R_{180°} = \begin{bmatrix} -1 & 0 \\ 0 & -1 \end{bmatrix}$; $R_{270°} = \begin{bmatrix} 0 & 1 \\ -1 & 0 \end{bmatrix}$

4.   (a) $\begin{bmatrix} 1 \\ 0 \end{bmatrix} \longrightarrow \begin{bmatrix} \cos 2\theta \\ \sin 2\theta \end{bmatrix}$, $\begin{bmatrix} 0 \\ 1 \end{bmatrix} \rightarrow \begin{bmatrix} \sin 2\theta \\ -\cos 2\theta \end{bmatrix}$

       (b) $\begin{bmatrix} \cos 2\theta & \sin 2\theta \\ \sin 2\theta & -\cos 2\theta \end{bmatrix}$

       (c) Reflection in x-axis, $(\theta = 0)$ $\begin{bmatrix} 1 & 0 \\ 0 & -1 \end{bmatrix}$

            Reflection in $y = -x$, $(\theta = 135°)$ $\begin{bmatrix} 0 & -1 \\ -1 & 0 \end{bmatrix}$

Matrices and trigonometric identities

1.   (a)   Addition of angles is commutative, $\theta + \phi = \phi + \theta$

(b) $\mathbf{R}_\theta = \begin{bmatrix} \cos\theta & -\sin\theta \\ \sin\theta & \cos\theta \end{bmatrix}$, $\mathbf{R}_\phi = \begin{bmatrix} \cos\phi & -\sin\phi \\ \sin\phi & \cos\phi \end{bmatrix}$

$\mathbf{R}_\theta \mathbf{R}_\phi = \begin{bmatrix} \cos\theta\cos\phi - \sin\theta\sin\phi & -(\sin\theta\cos\phi + \cos\theta\sin\phi) \\ \sin\theta\cos\phi + \cos\theta\sin\phi & \cos\theta\cos\phi - \sin\theta\sin\phi \end{bmatrix}$

(c)   A rotation about (0, 0) through $\theta + \phi$

(d)   The matrix for (c) is $\begin{bmatrix} \cos(\phi + \theta) & -\sin(\theta + \phi) \\ \sin(\theta + \phi) & \cos(\theta + \phi) \end{bmatrix}$. Compare with (b).

(e) $\sin(\theta + \phi) = \sin\theta\cos\phi + \cos\theta\sin\phi$

2.   (a) $\mathbf{R}_{-\theta}\mathbf{R}_\theta$ means rotate θ in one direction and then θ in the opposite direction. The net result is no change.

(b)   From the graphs

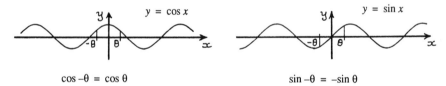

$\cos-\theta = \cos\theta$ $\sin-\theta = -\sin\theta$

(c) $\mathbf{R}_{-\theta} = \begin{bmatrix} \cos\theta & \sin\theta \\ -\sin\theta & \cos\theta \end{bmatrix}$

(d) $\mathbf{R}_{-\theta}\mathbf{R}_\theta = \begin{bmatrix} \cos^2\theta + \sin^2\theta & 0 \\ 0 & \cos^2\theta + \sin^2\theta \end{bmatrix}$

From (a), $\mathbf{R}_{-\theta}\mathbf{R}_\theta = \mathbf{I}$ and so $\cos^2\theta + \sin^2\theta = 1$

3.   (a) $\mathbf{M}_\theta = \begin{bmatrix} \cos2\theta & \sin2\theta \\ \sin2\theta & -\cos2\theta \end{bmatrix}$

(b) $\mathbf{M}_\theta^2 = \begin{bmatrix} 1 & 0 \\ 0 & 1 \end{bmatrix} = \mathbf{I}$. All reflections are self-inverse.

Inverse transformations

1. (a) $\begin{bmatrix} p & q \\ r & s \end{bmatrix}\begin{bmatrix} 4 & 1 \\ 3 & 2 \end{bmatrix} = \begin{bmatrix} 1 & 0 \\ 0 & 1 \end{bmatrix} \Rightarrow \begin{bmatrix} 4p + 3q & p + 2q \\ 4r + 3s & r + 2s \end{bmatrix} = \begin{bmatrix} 1 & 0 \\ 0 & 1 \end{bmatrix}$

    Comparing top rows, $4p + 3q = 1$, $p + 2q = 0$.

    (b) $p = \frac{2}{5}$, $q = -\frac{1}{5}$

    (c) $4r + 3s = 0$, $r + 2s = 1 \Rightarrow r = \frac{-3}{5}$, $s = \frac{4}{5}$

    (d) $\mathbf{M}^{-1} = \begin{bmatrix} p & q \\ r & s \end{bmatrix} = \begin{bmatrix} \frac{2}{5} & \frac{-1}{5} \\ \frac{-3}{5} & \frac{4}{5} \end{bmatrix} = \frac{1}{5}\begin{bmatrix} 2 & -1 \\ -3 & 4 \end{bmatrix}$

    (f) $\mathbf{M}(P) = \begin{bmatrix} -3 \\ 4 \end{bmatrix}$ and $\mathbf{M}^{-1}\begin{bmatrix} -3 \\ 4 \end{bmatrix} = \begin{bmatrix} -2 \\ 5 \end{bmatrix}$

2. The inverse matrix is $\frac{1}{8}\begin{bmatrix} 2 & 1 \\ 2 & 5 \end{bmatrix}$

3. (a) $\begin{bmatrix} p & q \\ r & s \end{bmatrix}\begin{bmatrix} a & b \\ c & d \end{bmatrix} = \begin{bmatrix} ap + cq & bp + dq \\ ar + cs & br + ds \end{bmatrix} = \begin{bmatrix} 1 & 0 \\ 0 & 1 \end{bmatrix}$

    Top row, $ap + cq = 1$, $bp + dq = 0$

    (c) $ar + cs = 0$, $br + ds = 1$

    $r = \frac{-c}{ab - bc}$; $s = \frac{a}{ad - bc}$

    (f) The inverse of $\begin{bmatrix} 2 & -5 \\ 1 & 2 \end{bmatrix}$ is $\frac{1}{9}\begin{bmatrix} 2 & 5 \\ -1 & 2 \end{bmatrix}$

4. (a) $\overrightarrow{OC} = \begin{bmatrix} a + b \\ c + d \end{bmatrix}$

    (b) Area $ODCE = (a + b)(c + d)$

    (c) Areas of the triangles are $\frac{1}{2}ac$, $\frac{1}{2}bd$, $\frac{1}{2}ac$, $\frac{1}{2}bd$. Areas of the rectangles are bc, bc.

    (d) Area of the parallelogram

    $= (a + b)(c + d) - ac - bd - 2bc$
    $= ac + bc + ad + bd - ac - bd - 2bc$
    $= ad - bc$

(continued)

5.　　(a)　(i)　Enlargement, centre $(0, 0)$, scale factor 2

　　　　　(ii)　Shear, Ox invariant, $(0, 1) \rightarrow (2, 1)$.

　　　　　(iii)　Rotation about $(0, 0)$ through $270°$.

　　　　　(iv)　Two-way stretch, factors 2, 3 along Ox, Oy.

(b)

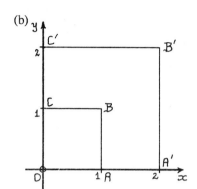 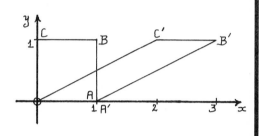

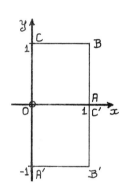 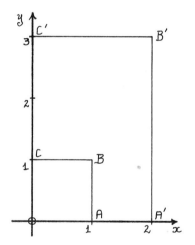

　　(c)　(i)　Determinant = 4, area $OA'B'C'$ = 2 x 2 = 4

　　　　　(ii)　Determinant = 1, area $OA'B'C'$ = base x height = 1 x 1 = 1

　　　　　(iii)　Determinant = 1, area $OA'B'C'$ = 1

　　　　　(iii)　Determinant = 6, area $OA'B'C'$ = 2 x 3 = 6.

6.　　(a)　-1, -1, -1, -1.

　　(b)　The area factor is 1 in each case. The determinant is negative because the transformations are reflections.

Linear transformations

1.   (a) $\begin{bmatrix} 1 \\ 8 \end{bmatrix}$, $\begin{bmatrix} 2 \\ 16 \end{bmatrix}$, $\begin{bmatrix} 3 \\ 24 \end{bmatrix}$, $\begin{bmatrix} 0 \\ 0 \end{bmatrix}$, $\begin{bmatrix} -1 \\ -8 \end{bmatrix}$, $\begin{bmatrix} -2 \\ -16 \end{bmatrix}$ They lie on a straight line.

    (b) $\begin{bmatrix} 11 \\ 3 \end{bmatrix}$, $\begin{bmatrix} 22 \\ 6 \end{bmatrix}$, $\begin{bmatrix} 33 \\ 9 \end{bmatrix}$, $\begin{bmatrix} 0 \\ 0 \end{bmatrix}$, $\begin{bmatrix} -11 \\ -3 \end{bmatrix}$, $\begin{bmatrix} -22 \\ -6 \end{bmatrix}$ They lie on a straight line.

2.   (a) (i) $\begin{bmatrix} px + qy \\ rx + sy \end{bmatrix}$ (ii) $\begin{bmatrix} p\lambda x + q\lambda y \\ r\lambda x + s\lambda y \end{bmatrix}$

    (b) $\lambda \begin{bmatrix} px + qy \\ rx + sy \end{bmatrix} = \lambda\,\mathbf{T(a)} = \begin{bmatrix} p\lambda x + q\lambda y \\ r\lambda x + s\lambda y \end{bmatrix} = \mathbf{T}(\lambda \mathbf{a})$

    (c) Lines through $(0, 0)$ are transformed to lines through $(0, 0)$.

    (d) The origin maps to itself.

3.   (a) (i) $\begin{bmatrix} px_1 + qy_1 \\ rx_1 + sy_1 \end{bmatrix}$ (ii) $\begin{bmatrix} px_2 + qy_2 \\ rx_2 + sy_2 \end{bmatrix}$ (iii) $\begin{bmatrix} p(x_1 + x_2) + q(y_1 + y_2) \\ r(x_1 + x_2) + s(y_1 + y_2) \end{bmatrix}$

    (b) $\mathbf{T\,(a + b)} = \begin{bmatrix} p(x_1 + x_2) + q(y_1 + y_2) \\ r(x_1 + x_2) + s(y_1 + y_2) \end{bmatrix} = \begin{bmatrix} px_1 + qy_1 \\ rx_1 + sy_1 \end{bmatrix} + \begin{bmatrix} px_2 + qy_2 \\ rx_2 + sy_2 \end{bmatrix} = \mathbf{T\,(a)} + \mathbf{T\,(b)}$

4.

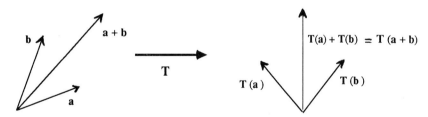

It does not matter whether you add the vectors then transform them or transform the vectors and then add their images.

5.   (a) $\mathbf{T\,(i)} = \begin{bmatrix} 3 \\ 1 \end{bmatrix}$, $\mathbf{T\,(j)} = \begin{bmatrix} 2 \\ 1 \end{bmatrix}$ $\mathbf{T(r)} = \begin{bmatrix} 21 \\ 8 \end{bmatrix} = 5\begin{bmatrix} 3 \\ 1 \end{bmatrix} + 3\begin{bmatrix} 2 \\ 1 \end{bmatrix}$

    (b) $\mathbf{T\,(i)} = \begin{bmatrix} 1 \\ -1 \end{bmatrix}$, $\mathbf{T\,(j)} = \begin{bmatrix} 1 \\ 1 \end{bmatrix}$ $\mathbf{T(r)} = \begin{bmatrix} 8 \\ -2 \end{bmatrix} = 5\begin{bmatrix} 1 \\ -1 \end{bmatrix} + 3\begin{bmatrix} 1 \\ 1 \end{bmatrix}$

    (c) $\mathbf{T\,(i)} = \begin{bmatrix} 2 \\ 0 \end{bmatrix}$, $\mathbf{T\,(j)} = \begin{bmatrix} 5 \\ -3 \end{bmatrix}$ $\mathbf{T(r)} = \begin{bmatrix} 25 \\ -9 \end{bmatrix} = 5\begin{bmatrix} 2 \\ 0 \end{bmatrix} + 3\begin{bmatrix} 5 \\ -3 \end{bmatrix}$.

6. $\mathbf{T}\,(x\,\mathbf{i} + y\,\mathbf{j}) = \mathbf{T}\,(x\,\mathbf{i}) + T\,(y\,\mathbf{j})$ (linearity)
                      $= x\,\mathbf{T}\,(\mathbf{i}) + y\,\mathbf{T}\,(\mathbf{j})$ (linearity)
     The point (x, y) on the square grid is transformed to the point (x, y) on the parallelogram grid.

1. (a) **A** : reflection in $y = x$
        B : 90° anti-clockwise rotation about (0,0)

    (b) $\mathbf{AB} = \begin{bmatrix} 1 & 0 \\ 0 & -1 \end{bmatrix}$ $\mathbf{BA} = \begin{bmatrix} -1 & 0 \\ 0 & 1 \end{bmatrix}$

    (c) **AB** : reflection in $y = 0$ (the x-axis)
        BA : reflection in $x = 0$ (the y-axis)

    (d) $|\mathbf{A}| = -1$; $|\mathbf{B}| = -1$
        The numerical value of 1 means the area is invariant ; the negative sign indicates the transformation is a reflection.

    (e) $\mathbf{A}^{-1} = \mathbf{A}$ $\mathbf{B}^{-1} = \mathbf{B}$

2. (a) $\begin{bmatrix} 2 & 0 \\ 0 & 2.5 \end{bmatrix}$ (b) $\begin{bmatrix} 1 & 0 \\ -2 & 1 \end{bmatrix}$ (c) $\begin{bmatrix} -0.5 & -0.87 \\ 0.87 & -0.5 \end{bmatrix}$ (d) $\begin{bmatrix} 0.6 & 0.8 \\ 0.8 & -0.6 \end{bmatrix}$

3. (a) Two-way stretch, scale factor 0.5 in the x direction and 0.4 in the y direction.
        $\begin{bmatrix} 0.5 & 0 \\ 0 & 0.4 \end{bmatrix}$

    (b) A shear with y-axis invariant and $(1, 0) \rightarrow (1, 2)$. $\begin{bmatrix} 1 & 0 \\ 2 & 1 \end{bmatrix}$

    (c) A rotation of 120° clockwise about the origin. $\begin{bmatrix} -0.5 & 0.87 \\ -0.87 & -0.5 \end{bmatrix}$

    (d) Reflection in $y = 0.5x$ (self-inverse). $\begin{bmatrix} 0.6 & 0.8 \\ 0.8 & -0.6 \end{bmatrix}$

4. (a) 3, $\frac{1}{3}\begin{bmatrix} 2 & -1 \\ -1 & 2 \end{bmatrix}$ (b) -1, $\begin{bmatrix} -1 & -2 \\ -2 & -3 \end{bmatrix}$ (c) 1, $\begin{bmatrix} 0.6 & 0.8 \\ -0.8 & 0.6 \end{bmatrix}$ (d) -1, $\begin{bmatrix} 0.6 & -0.8 \\ -0.8 & -0.6 \end{bmatrix}$

5. (a) $\mathbf{T}(\lambda\, \mathbf{a}) = \lambda\, \mathbf{T}(\mathbf{a})$ $\left.\phantom{\begin{matrix} 1 \\ 1 \end{matrix}}\right\}$ for any vectors **a**, **b** and any real number λ.
    (b) $\mathbf{T}(\mathbf{a} + \mathbf{b}) = \mathbf{T}(\mathbf{a}) + \mathbf{T}(\mathbf{b})$

6. (a), (d) are linear ; (b) , (c) are non-linear.

7. Translations do not leave the origin invariant.

8. (a) **A** : reflection in the plane $x = z$; **B** : reflection in the plane $x = -z$.

    (b) $\mathbf{AB} = \mathbf{BA} = \begin{bmatrix} -1 & 0 & 0 \\ 0 & 1 & 0 \\ 0 & 0 & -1 \end{bmatrix}$

    (c) **AB** and **BA** : rotation of 180° about y-axis.

3 Simultaneous equations

3.1 Introduction

(a) What point is transformed by the matrix $\begin{bmatrix} 1 & 2 \\ 1 & -1 \end{bmatrix}$ into the point (5, 2)?

(b) What alternative method of solving simultaneous equations is suggested by your answer to (a)?

(c) What are the practical advantages and disadvantages of the methods available for solving a pair of simultaneous equations?

(a) If **T** is the transformation with matrix $\begin{bmatrix} 1 & 2 \\ 1 & -1 \end{bmatrix}$

then $(x, y) \xrightarrow{\quad \textbf{T} \quad} (5, 2)$.
$\xleftarrow{\quad \textbf{T}^{-1} \quad}$

So
$$\begin{bmatrix} x \\ y \end{bmatrix} = \textbf{T}^{-1} \begin{bmatrix} 5 \\ 2 \end{bmatrix}$$

$$\Rightarrow \quad \begin{bmatrix} x \\ y \end{bmatrix} = \frac{1}{-1-2} \begin{bmatrix} -1 & -2 \\ -1 & 1 \end{bmatrix} \begin{bmatrix} 5 \\ 2 \end{bmatrix}$$

$$\Rightarrow \quad \begin{bmatrix} x \\ y \end{bmatrix} = -\frac{1}{3} \begin{bmatrix} -9 \\ -3 \end{bmatrix} = \begin{bmatrix} 3 \\ 1 \end{bmatrix}$$

The original point is (3,1).

(b) A possible method is therefore to

• rearrange the equations in the form

$$\begin{matrix} a_1 x + b_1 y = c_1 \\ a_2 x + b_2 y = c_2 \end{matrix} \quad \Rightarrow \begin{bmatrix} a_1 & b_1 \\ a_2 & b_2 \end{bmatrix} \begin{bmatrix} x \\ y \end{bmatrix} = \begin{bmatrix} c_1 \\ c_2 \end{bmatrix}$$

• calculate $\begin{bmatrix} x \\ y \end{bmatrix} = \begin{bmatrix} a_1 & b_1 \\ a_2 & b_2 \end{bmatrix}^{-1} \begin{bmatrix} c_1 \\ c_2 \end{bmatrix}$

(c) **Geometry**

Advantages

•   The method is very simple and easy to understand.

Disadvantages

•   It is time-consuming.
•   It is inaccurate if the solutions are not whole numbers or simple fractions.

Elimination

Advantages

•   The method extends easily to equations with more than 2 variables.

•   With a good choice of row multiples this is usually the quickest method.

Disadvantages

•   Non-integral coefficients make the working messy.

•   Some problems require geometrical insight.

Inverse matrix

Advantages

•   The method is always the same.

•   It extends to equations with more than 2 variables.

Disadvantages

•   For equations with a large number of variables elimination is the best method of finding the inverse matrix.

•   Not all matrices have inverses.

For solving simultaneous equations, the method of elimination is usually preferred. However, useful geometrical insights can arise both by considering geometrical intersections and by considering transformation matrices.

Elimination

1. (a) $2x + 5y = 11$ ①
         $3x + y = 10$ ②

         $5② - ①,$ $13x = 39$
                   $\Rightarrow$ $x = 3$
         In ②, $y = 1$

    (b) $x - 3y = -4$ ①
         $2x + 3y = 1$ ②

         $① + ②,$ $3x = -3$
                   $\Rightarrow x = -1$
         In ②, $y = 1$

    (c) $2x - 3y = 4$ ①
         $3x - 4y = 6$ ②

         $3① - 2②$ $-17y = 0$
                   $\Rightarrow$ $y = 0$
         In ①, $x = 2$

    (d) Rearrange to give
         $5x - 2y = -4$ ①
         $3x - y = -1$ ②

         $① - 2②,$ $-x = -2$
                   $\Rightarrow$ $x = 2$

         In ②, $y = 7$

    (e) Rearrange to give
         $-4x + 2y = 1$ ①
         $5x + 3y = 7$ ②

         $2② - 3①,$ $22x = 11$
                   $\Rightarrow$ $x = 0.5$

         In ①, $y = 1.5$

2. $3y = 1 + 2x$ $\Rightarrow$ $-2x + 3y = 1$ ①
    $7y = 5x + 3$ $\Rightarrow$ $-5x + 7y = 3$ ②

    $2② - 5①,$ $\Rightarrow$ $-y = 1$
                            $y = -1$

    In ①, $x = -2$

Destroying a dimension

1.   (a) $A' = \mathbf{T}(A)$

$$= \begin{bmatrix} -1 & -3 \\ 2 & -1 \end{bmatrix} \begin{bmatrix} 1 & 4 & 4 & 1 \\ 1 & 1 & -1 & -1 \end{bmatrix}$$

$$= \begin{bmatrix} -4 & -7 & -1 & 2 \\ 1 & 7 & 9 & 3 \end{bmatrix}$$

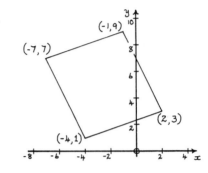

    (b)   (i)   Area of A = 6 square units

           (ii)   Area of A' = 42 square units

           (iii) $|\mathbf{T}| = 1 - (-6) = 7$

        Multiplying the area of A by $|\mathbf{T}|$ gives the area of A'.
        i.e. $|\mathbf{T}|$ is the **area scale factor** of the transformation.

2.   (a) $B' = \mathbf{S}(B) = \begin{bmatrix} 2 & -1 \\ -4 & 2 \end{bmatrix} \begin{bmatrix} 1 & 1 & -3 & -6 & -2 \\ 5 & 2 & -4 & -1 & 5 \end{bmatrix} = \begin{bmatrix} -3 & 0 & -2 & -11 & -9 \\ 6 & 0 & 4 & 22 & 18 \end{bmatrix}$

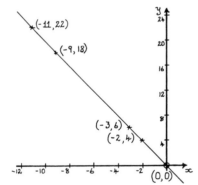

    (b)   Area of **S**   = 34.5

        Area of **S'**   = 0
        $|\mathbf{S}| = 4 - 4$ = 0

        So $|\mathbf{S}|$ is the area scale factor of the transformation.

    (c)   Any 2-dimensional object will be crushed onto the line $y = -2x$.

3.   (a)   All points are transformed onto points satisfying $y = -2x$.
    (b) $|\mathbf{R}| = 4 - 4 = 0$
    (c)   The image space of **R** is the line given by $y = -2x$.
    (d)   The (x, y) plane has been crushed onto a line, and so the dimension of the image
        space is one less than that of the original plane.

1. (a) $x = \dfrac{9a - 48}{ab - 16}$, $y = \dfrac{6b - 18}{ab - 16}$

    (b) If $ab \neq 16$ the solution is unique.

        If $ab = 16$ there are no solutions unless $6b = 18$ and $9a = 48$.

        If $a = \dfrac{16}{3}$ and $b = 3$, there are an infinite number of solutions.

2. $|A| = 0$ so the matrix represents a crushing transformation.

    If $(x, y) \rightarrow (x', y')$, then

    $$\begin{bmatrix} x' \\ y' \end{bmatrix} = \begin{bmatrix} 3 & 2 \\ 6 & 4 \end{bmatrix} \begin{bmatrix} x \\ y \end{bmatrix} = \begin{bmatrix} 3x + 2y \\ 6x + 4y \end{bmatrix}$$

    $\Rightarrow y' = 2x'$ and so the image space is the line $y = 2x$.

3. $3x - y = 9$

    $2x - 4y = 16$

    have solution $x = 2$, $y = -3$.

    Then $5x + 2y = 10 - 6 = 4$ and a must equal 4 for the set of equations to be consistent. If $a = 4$, the equations have solution $x = 2$, $y = -3$.

    If $a \neq 4$ the equations are inconsistent and have no solution.

4. (a) $x = 3$, $y = -2$, $z = 5$

    (b) $x = \dfrac{5}{4} - \dfrac{7}{2}\lambda$, $y = 4\lambda$, $z = -\dfrac{3}{2} - 13\lambda$

        There are many alternative expressions.

(continued)

5. $2x - y + 5z = 7$ ①

         $5x + 3y - z = 4$ ②

         $3x + 4y - 6z = k$ ③

         $5 \times ① - 2 \times ②, \quad -11y + 27z = 27$

         $3 \times ① - 2 \times ③, \quad -11y + 27z = 21 - 2k$

         For the planes to form a sheaf, $21 - 2k = 27$

                                     $\Rightarrow \quad\quad k = -3$

6. $x + y = a$ ①

         $y + z = b$ ②

         $z - x = c$ ③

         $① - ② + ③, \quad 0 = a - b + c$

         The planes form a prism if $a - b + c \neq 0$.

7.   The planes $3x - y + 2z = 0$ and $6x - 2y + 4z = 5$ are parallel.

         The plane $x + 4x + 3y = 2$ is not parallel to the other planes and so intersects both of them.

36

4 *Identifying transformations*

4.1 Introduction

> (a) By illustrating the effect of the matrix $A = \begin{bmatrix} 1 & 0 \\ 0 & -1 \end{bmatrix}$ on the unit vectors **i** and **j**, describe the transformation represented by A.
>
> (b) Illustrate the effect of the matrix $B = \begin{bmatrix} -1 & 2 \\ -2 & 3 \end{bmatrix}$ on the unit vectors **i** and **j**. Why is it not easy to determine the transformation represented by B?
>
> (c) What else could you investigate to help discover the geometrical effects of B?
>
> (d) How would it help if you knew that certain points or lines are fixed? How could you find these?

(a) $\mathbf{i} \to \mathbf{i}, \ \mathbf{j} \to -\mathbf{j}$.

The transformation represented by **A** is a reflection in the *x*-axis.

(b) $\mathbf{i} \to -\mathbf{i} - 2\mathbf{j}, \ \mathbf{j} \to 2\mathbf{i} + 3\mathbf{j}$.

Transformations can only be easily recognised from their matrices when the transformation has a simple effect on the base vectors **i** and **j**.

(c) The determinant can be useful. For example,

$$\begin{vmatrix} -1 & 2 \\ -2 & 3 \end{vmatrix} = -3 + 4 = 1$$

and so the transformation has area scale factor 1. It is especially useful to consider the fixed points and lines, as in (d).

(d) (i) Transformations have various numbers of fixed points:
   - a rotation fixes precisely one point;
   - a reflection fixes a whole line of points;
   - a two-way stretch fixes two lines although only one point is actually fixed.

   Knowing the fixed points and/or lines can therefore be very useful.

   (ii) To find a fixed point **a** you must solve the matrix equation

   $$\mathbf{Ba} = \mathbf{a}.$$

   To find a fixed line through **a** you must solve the equation

   $$\mathbf{Ba} = \lambda \mathbf{a}.$$

   This chapter deals with the solution of such equations.

Finding clues

1.   (a) $|M| = 1$ and so the area is unchanged by the transformation. The transformation cannot therefore be an enlargement, for example.

(b) $(3, 1) \rightarrow (-1, -3)$ $(7, 7) \rightarrow (7, 7)$
      $(-2, -2) \rightarrow (-2, -2)$ $(3, 5) \rightarrow (7, 9)$
      $(4, 1) \rightarrow (-2, -5)$

(c) $(-2, -2)$ and $(7, 7)$ are invariant points

(d) $\begin{bmatrix} -1 & 2 \\ -2 & 3 \end{bmatrix} \begin{bmatrix} x \\ y \end{bmatrix} = \begin{bmatrix} x \\ y \end{bmatrix} \Rightarrow \begin{matrix} -x + 2y = x \\ -2x + 3y = y \end{matrix} \} \Rightarrow y = x$

All points on the line $y = x$ are invariant.

(e)   (i)   A rotation has only one fixed point.

(ii)   An enlargement has determinant $\neq 1$ and only one invariant point.

(iii)   A two-way stretch has only one invariant point.

(f)   **M** is a shear with $y = x$ as the invariant line.

2.   (a) $M \begin{bmatrix} 0 \\ 0 \end{bmatrix} = \begin{bmatrix} 0 \\ 0 \end{bmatrix}$ for any **M**.

(b) $\begin{bmatrix} 0 \\ 0 \end{bmatrix} + \begin{bmatrix} a \\ b \end{bmatrix} = \begin{bmatrix} a \\ b \end{bmatrix}$.   The origin is not invariant under a translation and therefore a translation cannot be represented by a transformation matrix.

(c)   The centre of rotation must be at the origin.

(d)   The mirror line must pass through the origin.

(e)   The area scale factor for a rotation is 1 and for a reflection is -1

These are the values of the corresponding determinants.

3.   (a) $\begin{bmatrix} -0.6 & 0.8 \\ 0.8 & 0.6 \end{bmatrix} \begin{bmatrix} t \\ 2t \end{bmatrix} = \begin{bmatrix} t \\ 2t \end{bmatrix}$.   Points of the form $(t, 2t)$ are therefore invariant.

(b)   (i)   Rotation, enlargement, stretch   (ii)   Reflection, shear.

(c) $|M| = -1$. The matrix represents a reflection in $y = 2x$.

4. $\begin{bmatrix} 0.6 & -0.8 \\ -0.8 & -0.6 \end{bmatrix} \begin{bmatrix} 2t \\ -t \end{bmatrix} = \begin{bmatrix} 2t \\ -t \end{bmatrix}$

$|M| = -1$. The matrix represents a reflection in $y = -\dfrac{1}{2} x$.

Fixed directions

1.   (a) $(1, 1) \rightarrow (4, 4)$ $(5, 5) \rightarrow (20, 20)$ $(-7, -7) \rightarrow (-28, -28)$

       (b) $(t, t) \rightarrow (4t, 4t)$

            The line $\mathbf{r} = t \begin{bmatrix} 1 \\ 1 \end{bmatrix}$ is invariant. All points on this line are mapped onto points on the line by a stretch of factor 4.

       (c) $(3t, 2t) \rightarrow (9t, 6t)$

            $(9t, 6t)$ is on the line $\mathbf{r} = t \begin{bmatrix} 3 \\ 2 \end{bmatrix}$, so the line is invariant.

       (d)   **M** is a transformation with two fixed lines, involving stretches of factors 4 and 3 in their respective directions.

2.   (a) $\begin{bmatrix} -0.28 & 0.96 \\ 0.96 & 0.28 \end{bmatrix} \begin{bmatrix} 3t \\ 4t \end{bmatrix} = \begin{bmatrix} 3t \\ 4t \end{bmatrix}$

       (b) $\begin{bmatrix} -0.28 & 0.96 \\ 0.96 & 0.28 \end{bmatrix} \begin{bmatrix} -4t \\ 3t \end{bmatrix} = \begin{bmatrix} 4t \\ -3t \end{bmatrix} = \begin{bmatrix} -4t \\ 3t \end{bmatrix}$

       (c)   The transformation is a reflection with $\mathbf{r} = t \begin{bmatrix} 3 \\ 4 \end{bmatrix}$ as mirror line. Note that the line $\mathbf{r} = t \begin{bmatrix} -4 \\ 3 \end{bmatrix}$ is perpendicular to the mirror line and points on this line are stretched by a factor of -1.

3.   (a) $\begin{bmatrix} 0.8 & 0.4 \\ 0.4 & 0.2 \end{bmatrix} \begin{bmatrix} 2t \\ t \end{bmatrix} = \begin{bmatrix} 2t \\ t \end{bmatrix}$ $\begin{bmatrix} 0.8 & 0.4 \\ 0.4 & 0.2 \end{bmatrix} \begin{bmatrix} -t \\ 2t \end{bmatrix} = \begin{bmatrix} 0 \\ 0 \end{bmatrix}$

       (b)   The line $\mathbf{r} = t \begin{bmatrix} 2 \\ 1 \end{bmatrix}$ is a line of invariant points and the line $\mathbf{r} = t \begin{bmatrix} -1 \\ 2 \end{bmatrix}$ is projected onto the origin.

            The lines are perpendicular and the geometric effect is a perpendicular projection onto the line $\mathbf{r} = t \begin{bmatrix} 2 \\ 1 \end{bmatrix}$

Finding eigenvectors

1. (a) If $x = 3t$, $y = t$ then $x - 3y = 3t - 3t = 0$

$\begin{bmatrix} 3 \\ 1 \end{bmatrix}$, $\begin{bmatrix} 6 \\ 2 \end{bmatrix}$, $\begin{bmatrix} -6 \\ -2 \end{bmatrix}$ all satisfy $x - 3y = 0$

(b) $x = -\dfrac{5}{4}y \Rightarrow k = -\dfrac{5}{4}$

$\begin{bmatrix} -5 \\ 4 \end{bmatrix}$, $\begin{bmatrix} -\frac{35}{4} \\ 7 \end{bmatrix}$, $\begin{bmatrix} 5 \\ -4 \end{bmatrix}$ all satisfy $4x + 5y = 0$

(c) $\begin{bmatrix} -2 \\ 3 \end{bmatrix}$, $\begin{bmatrix} -4 \\ 6 \end{bmatrix}$, $\begin{bmatrix} 2 \\ -3 \end{bmatrix}$, etc.

2. (a) $\begin{bmatrix} 1 & -1 \\ 2 & 4 \end{bmatrix}\begin{bmatrix} x \\ y \end{bmatrix} = 2\begin{bmatrix} x \\ y \end{bmatrix} \Rightarrow \begin{matrix} x - y = 2x \\ 2x + 4y = 2y \end{matrix} \Rightarrow x + y = 0.$ An eigenvector is $\begin{bmatrix} 1 \\ -1 \end{bmatrix}$.

(b) $\begin{bmatrix} 1 & -1 \\ 2 & 4 \end{bmatrix}\begin{bmatrix} x \\ y \end{bmatrix} = 3\begin{bmatrix} x \\ y \end{bmatrix} \Rightarrow \begin{matrix} x - y = 3x \\ 2x + 4y = 3y \end{matrix} \Rightarrow 2x + y = 0.$ An eigenvector is $\begin{bmatrix} 1 \\ -2 \end{bmatrix}$.

(c) A two way stretch in directions $\begin{bmatrix} 1 \\ -1 \end{bmatrix}$ and $\begin{bmatrix} 1 \\ -2 \end{bmatrix}$ with factors 2 and 3 respectively.

3. $\begin{vmatrix} 2-\lambda & 3 \\ 4 & 1-\lambda \end{vmatrix} = 0 \Rightarrow (2 - \lambda)(1 - \lambda) - 12 = 0$

$\Rightarrow \quad \lambda^2 - 3\lambda - 10 = 0$

$\Rightarrow \quad (\lambda - 5)(\lambda + 2) = 0$

Eigenvalues –2, 5.

$\begin{bmatrix} 2 & 3 \\ 4 & 1 \end{bmatrix}\begin{bmatrix} x \\ y \end{bmatrix} = -2\begin{bmatrix} x \\ y \end{bmatrix} \quad \Rightarrow 4x + 3y = 0.$ An eigenvector is $\begin{bmatrix} 3 \\ -4 \end{bmatrix}$

$\begin{bmatrix} 2 & 3 \\ 4 & 1 \end{bmatrix}\begin{bmatrix} x \\ y \end{bmatrix} = 5\begin{bmatrix} x \\ y \end{bmatrix} \quad \Rightarrow x - y = 0.$ An eigenvector is $\begin{bmatrix} 1 \\ 1 \end{bmatrix}$

The matrix represents a two-way stretch in directions $\begin{bmatrix} 3 \\ -4 \end{bmatrix}$ and $\begin{bmatrix} 1 \\ 1 \end{bmatrix}$ with factors –2 and 5 respectively.

4. $\begin{vmatrix} 2-\lambda & -3 \\ 4 & 1-\lambda \end{vmatrix} = 0 \Rightarrow (2 - \lambda)(1 - \lambda) + 12 = 0$

$\Rightarrow \lambda^2 - 3\lambda + 14 = 0.$

The characteristic equation has no solutions. The transformation has no fixed lines.

Powers of a matrix

1. $\mathbf{M} = \mathbf{UDU^{-1}} \Rightarrow \mathbf{M^2} = (\mathbf{UDU^{-1}})\,(\mathbf{UDU^{-1}})$

$= \mathbf{UD^2U^{-1}}$, since $\mathbf{U^{-1}U} = \mathbf{I}$

$\mathbf{M^n} = \mathbf{UD^nU^{-1}}$

2. (a) $\begin{vmatrix} 4-\lambda & -3 \\ 2 & -1-\lambda \end{vmatrix} = 0 \Rightarrow (4-\lambda)(-1-\lambda) + 6 = 0$

$\Rightarrow \lambda^2 - 3\lambda + 2 = 0$

$\Rightarrow \lambda = 1,\ 2$

$\begin{bmatrix} 4 & -3 \\ 2 & -1 \end{bmatrix}\begin{bmatrix} x \\ y \end{bmatrix} = \begin{bmatrix} x \\ y \end{bmatrix} \quad \Rightarrow x - y = 0.$ An eigenvector is $\begin{bmatrix} 1 \\ 1 \end{bmatrix}$

$\begin{bmatrix} 4 & -3 \\ 2 & -1 \end{bmatrix}\begin{bmatrix} x \\ y \end{bmatrix} = 2\begin{bmatrix} x \\ y \end{bmatrix} \quad \Rightarrow 2x - 3y = 0.$ An eigenvector is $\begin{bmatrix} 3 \\ 2 \end{bmatrix}$

(b) $\mathbf{M} = \begin{bmatrix} 1 & 3 \\ 1 & 2 \end{bmatrix}\begin{bmatrix} 1 & 0 \\ 0 & 2 \end{bmatrix}\begin{bmatrix} -2 & 3 \\ 1 & -1 \end{bmatrix}$

(c) $\mathbf{M^{54}} = \begin{bmatrix} 1 & 3 \\ 1 & 2 \end{bmatrix}\begin{bmatrix} 1 & 0 \\ 0 & 2^{54} \end{bmatrix}\begin{bmatrix} -2 & 3 \\ 1 & -1 \end{bmatrix} = \begin{bmatrix} 1 & 3\times2^{54} \\ 1 & 2^{55} \end{bmatrix}\begin{bmatrix} -2 & 3 \\ 1 & -1 \end{bmatrix} = \begin{bmatrix} -2+3\times2^{54} & 3-3\times2^{54} \\ -2+2^{55} & 3-2^{55} \end{bmatrix}$

3. (a) $\mathbf{M} = \begin{bmatrix} \frac{1}{2} & \frac{1}{3} \\ \frac{1}{2} & \frac{2}{3} \end{bmatrix}$ $\lambda = 1$, eigenvector $= \begin{bmatrix} 2 \\ 3 \end{bmatrix}$

$\lambda = \dfrac{1}{6}$, eigenvector $= \begin{bmatrix} 1 \\ -1 \end{bmatrix}$

$\mathbf{M} = \begin{bmatrix} 2 & 1 \\ 3 & -1 \end{bmatrix}\begin{bmatrix} 1 & 0 \\ 0 & \frac{1}{6} \end{bmatrix}\begin{bmatrix} 0.2 & 0.2 \\ 0.6 & -0.4 \end{bmatrix}$

(b) $\mathbf{D^n} \to \begin{bmatrix} 1 & 0 \\ 0 & 0 \end{bmatrix}$ as $n \to +\infty$

(c) $\mathbf{M^n} \to \begin{bmatrix} 2 & 1 \\ 3 & -1 \end{bmatrix}\begin{bmatrix} 1 & 0 \\ 0 & 0 \end{bmatrix}\begin{bmatrix} 0.2 & 0.2 \\ 0.6 & -0.4 \end{bmatrix}$

$\mathbf{M^n} \to \begin{bmatrix} 0.4 & 0.4 \\ 0.6 & 0.6 \end{bmatrix}$ as $n \to +\infty$

Transition matrices

1. (a) $(0.7 - \lambda)(0.8 - \lambda) - 0.06 = 0$

   $\Rightarrow \lambda^2 - 1.5\lambda + 0.5 = 0$

   $\Rightarrow \lambda = 1, \ 0.5$

   Eigenvectors $\begin{bmatrix} 2 \\ 3 \end{bmatrix}, \begin{bmatrix} 1 \\ -1 \end{bmatrix}$

   $\mathbf{T} = \begin{bmatrix} 2 & 1 \\ 3 & -1 \end{bmatrix} \begin{bmatrix} 1 & 0 \\ 0 & 0.5 \end{bmatrix} \begin{bmatrix} 0.2 & 0.2 \\ 0.6 & -0.4 \end{bmatrix}$

   (b) $\mathbf{D}^n = \begin{bmatrix} 1 & 0 \\ 0 & 0.5^n \end{bmatrix} \rightarrow \begin{bmatrix} 1 & 0 \\ 0 & 0 \end{bmatrix}$ as $n \rightarrow +\infty$

   (c) $\mathbf{T}^n \rightarrow \begin{bmatrix} 2 & 1 \\ 3 & -1 \end{bmatrix} \begin{bmatrix} 1 & 0 \\ 0 & 0 \end{bmatrix} \begin{bmatrix} 0.2 & 0.2 \\ 0.6 & -0.4 \end{bmatrix} = \begin{bmatrix} 2 & 0 \\ 3 & 0 \end{bmatrix} \begin{bmatrix} 0.2 & 0.2 \\ 0.6 & -0.4 \end{bmatrix} = \begin{bmatrix} 0.4 & 0.4 \\ 0.6 & 0.6 \end{bmatrix}$ as $n \rightarrow +\infty$

   $\mathbf{T}^n \begin{bmatrix} 1 \\ 0 \end{bmatrix} \rightarrow \begin{bmatrix} 0.4 & 0.4 \\ 0.6 & 0.6 \end{bmatrix} \begin{bmatrix} 1 \\ 0 \end{bmatrix} = \begin{bmatrix} 0.4 \\ 0.6 \end{bmatrix}$ as $n \rightarrow +\infty$

   (d) The probability that the 100th day is sunny is 0.4. The result is the same regardless of the weather on the first day.

2. $\mathbf{T} = \begin{array}{c} G \\ F \end{array} \begin{array}{c} G \quad F \\ \begin{bmatrix} 0.9 & 0.2 \\ 0.1 & 0.8 \end{bmatrix} \end{array}$ $(0.9 - \lambda)(0.8 - \lambda) - 0.02 = 0$

   $\Rightarrow \lambda = 1, \ 0.7.$ Eigenvectors $\begin{bmatrix} 2 \\ 1 \end{bmatrix}, \begin{bmatrix} 1 \\ -1 \end{bmatrix}$

   $\mathbf{T} = \begin{bmatrix} 2 & 1 \\ 1 & -1 \end{bmatrix} \begin{bmatrix} 1 & 0 \\ 0 & 0.7 \end{bmatrix} \begin{bmatrix} \frac{1}{3} & \frac{1}{3} \\ \frac{1}{3} & -\frac{2}{3} \end{bmatrix}$

   $\mathbf{T}^n \rightarrow \begin{bmatrix} 2 & 1 \\ 1 & -1 \end{bmatrix} \begin{bmatrix} 1 & 0 \\ 0 & 0 \end{bmatrix} \begin{bmatrix} \frac{1}{3} & \frac{1}{3} \\ \frac{1}{3} & -\frac{2}{3} \end{bmatrix} = \begin{bmatrix} 2 & 0 \\ 1 & 0 \end{bmatrix} \begin{bmatrix} \frac{1}{3} & \frac{1}{3} \\ \frac{1}{3} & -\frac{2}{3} \end{bmatrix} = \begin{bmatrix} \frac{2}{3} & \frac{2}{3} \\ \frac{1}{3} & \frac{1}{3} \end{bmatrix}$ as $n \rightarrow +\infty$

   long term probability that the disc is good is $\frac{2}{3}$.

3. The corresponding eigenvectors are in the direction of $\begin{bmatrix} 2 \\ 3 \end{bmatrix}$ and $\begin{bmatrix} 2 \\ 1 \end{bmatrix}$. In the form $\begin{bmatrix} a \\ b \end{bmatrix}$ with $a + b = 1$, these become $\begin{bmatrix} 0.4 \\ 0.6 \end{bmatrix}$ and $\begin{bmatrix} \frac{2}{3} \\ \frac{1}{3} \end{bmatrix}$ which correspond to the long term probabilities. It is possible to prove that this happens for all transition matrices. This is considered further on Tasksheet 7.

42

1.   (a) $(2 - \lambda)(4 - \lambda) + 3 = 0$

             $\Rightarrow \lambda^2 - 6\lambda + 11 = 0$

        (b) $\mathbf{M}^2 - 6\mathbf{M} + 11\mathbf{I} = \begin{bmatrix} 1 & -6 \\ 18 & 13 \end{bmatrix} - \begin{bmatrix} 12 & -6 \\ 18 & 24 \end{bmatrix} + \begin{bmatrix} 11 & 0 \\ 0 & 11 \end{bmatrix} = \begin{bmatrix} 0 & 0 \\ 0 & 0 \end{bmatrix}$

2. $\mathbf{M}$ has characteristic equation $a\lambda^2 + b\lambda + c = 0$

        (a) λ_1 and λ_2 are eigenvalues of $\mathbf{M}$ and hence both satisfy the characteristic equation, giving

             $a\lambda_1^{\,2} + b\lambda_1 + c = 0$ and $a\lambda_2^{\,2} + b\lambda_2 + c = 0$

        (b) $\mathbf{D} = \begin{bmatrix} \lambda_1 & 0 \\ 0 & \lambda_2 \end{bmatrix}$, $\mathbf{D}^2 = \begin{bmatrix} \lambda_1^2 & 0 \\ 0 & \lambda_2^2 \end{bmatrix}$, $a\mathbf{D}^2 + b\mathbf{D} + c\mathbf{I} = \begin{bmatrix} a\lambda_1^2 + b\lambda_1 + c & 0 \\ 0 & a\lambda_2^2 + b\lambda_2 + c \end{bmatrix} = \mathbf{0}$

        (c) $a\mathbf{M}^2 + b\mathbf{M} + c\mathbf{I} = a\,(\mathbf{UDU}^{-1})^2 + b\,(\mathbf{UDU}^{-1}) + c\mathbf{I}$

                                $= a\,\mathbf{UD}^2\mathbf{U}^{-1} + b\mathbf{UDU}^{-1} + c\mathbf{UIU}^{-1}$, since $\mathbf{UIU}^{-1} = \mathbf{UU}^{-1} = \mathbf{I}$

                                $= \mathbf{U}(a\mathbf{D}^2 + b\mathbf{D} + c\mathbf{I})\mathbf{U}^{-1}$

                                $= \mathbf{0}$, since $a\mathbf{D}^2 + b\mathbf{D} + c\mathbf{I} = \mathbf{0}$

3.   (a) $\mathbf{M}^2 - 3\mathbf{M} + 5\mathbf{I} = \begin{bmatrix} 1 & -3 \\ 9 & -2 \end{bmatrix} - \begin{bmatrix} 6 & -3 \\ 9 & 3 \end{bmatrix} + \begin{bmatrix} 5 & 0 \\ 0 & 5 \end{bmatrix} = \begin{bmatrix} 0 & 0 \\ 0 & 0 \end{bmatrix} = \mathbf{0}$

        (b) $\mathbf{M}^{-1}\,(\mathbf{M}^2 - 3\mathbf{M} + 5\mathbf{I}) = \mathbf{M}^{-1}\,\mathbf{0}$

             $\Rightarrow \mathbf{M} - 3\mathbf{I} + 5\mathbf{M}^{-1} = \mathbf{0}$

             $\Rightarrow \mathbf{M}^{-1} = \frac{1}{5}\,(3\mathbf{I} - \mathbf{M}) = \frac{1}{5}\left(\begin{bmatrix} 3 & 0 \\ 0 & 3 \end{bmatrix} - \begin{bmatrix} 2 & -1 \\ 3 & 1 \end{bmatrix}\right) = \begin{bmatrix} 0.2 & 0.2 \\ -0.6 & 0.4 \end{bmatrix}$

        (c) $\mathbf{M}^{-1}\,\mathbf{M} = \begin{bmatrix} 0.2 & 0.2 \\ -0.6 & 0.4 \end{bmatrix}\begin{bmatrix} 2 & -1 \\ 3 & 1 \end{bmatrix} = \begin{bmatrix} 1 & 0 \\ 0 & 1 \end{bmatrix}$

(continued)

(d) $\mathbf{M}^2 = 3\mathbf{M} - 5\mathbf{I}$

$$= \begin{bmatrix} 6 & -3 \\ 9 & 3 \end{bmatrix} - \begin{bmatrix} 5 & 0 \\ 0 & 5 \end{bmatrix}$$

$$= \begin{bmatrix} 1 & -3 \\ 9 & -2 \end{bmatrix}$$

(e) $\mathbf{M}^2 - 3\mathbf{M} + 5\mathbf{I} = 0 \quad \Rightarrow (\mathbf{M}^2 - 3\mathbf{M} + 5\mathbf{I})\mathbf{M} = 0$
$$\Rightarrow \mathbf{M}^3 - 3\mathbf{M}^2 + 5\mathbf{M} = 0$$

$\mathbf{M}^3 = 3\mathbf{M}^2 - 5\mathbf{M}$

$$= \begin{bmatrix} 3 & -9 \\ 27 & -6 \end{bmatrix} - \begin{bmatrix} 10 & -5 \\ 15 & 5 \end{bmatrix}$$

$$= \begin{bmatrix} -7 & -4 \\ 12 & -11 \end{bmatrix}$$

4.   (a) $\begin{vmatrix} 2-\lambda & -1 \\ 3 & 4-\lambda \end{vmatrix} = 0$

$\Rightarrow \lambda^2 - 6\lambda + 11 = 0$

$\mathbf{M}^2 - 6\mathbf{M} + 11\mathbf{I} = 0$

$\Rightarrow \mathbf{M} - 6\mathbf{I} + 11\mathbf{M}^{-1} = 0$

$\Rightarrow \mathbf{M}^{-1} = \frac{1}{11}(6\mathbf{I} - \mathbf{M}) = \frac{1}{11}\begin{bmatrix} 4 & 1 \\ -3 & 2 \end{bmatrix}$

(b) $\mathbf{M}^2 = 6\mathbf{M} - 11\mathbf{I} = \begin{bmatrix} 1 & -6 \\ 18 & 13 \end{bmatrix}$

$\mathbf{M}^3 = 6\mathbf{M}^2 - 11\mathbf{M} = \begin{bmatrix} 6 & -36 \\ 108 & 78 \end{bmatrix} - \begin{bmatrix} 22 & -11 \\ 33 & 44 \end{bmatrix} = \begin{bmatrix} -16 & -25 \\ 75 & 34 \end{bmatrix}$

1.   (a)   Each column represents the probability of each of the two events occurring subsequently, given that a particular state is occurring at present. The entries are therefore non-negative numbers.

For example, in the matrix $\begin{array}{cc} & \begin{array}{cc} S & C \end{array} \\ \begin{array}{c} S \\ C \end{array} & \begin{bmatrix} 0.7 & 0.2 \\ 0.3 & 0.8 \end{bmatrix} \end{array}$ the first column represents the

probabilities that it will be sunny (S) or cloudy (C) tomorrow if it is sunny today. Since one or other state must occur, the probabilities sum to 1.

(b) $\begin{vmatrix} 1-a-\lambda & b \\ \\ a & 1-b-\lambda \end{vmatrix} = 0 \Rightarrow (1-a-\lambda)(1-b-\lambda) - ab = 0$

$$\Rightarrow (\lambda - 1)(\lambda - 1 + a + b) = 0$$

$$\Rightarrow \lambda_1 = 1 \text{ and } \lambda_2 = 1 - a - b$$

$0 \leq a, b \leq 1 \Rightarrow 0 \leq a + b \leq 2 \Rightarrow |\lambda_2| \leq 1$

(c) $\begin{bmatrix} 1-a & b \\ a & 1-b \end{bmatrix} \begin{bmatrix} x \\ y \end{bmatrix} = \lambda \begin{bmatrix} x \\ y \end{bmatrix} \Rightarrow (1-a)x + by = \lambda x$

$\lambda = 1 \Rightarrow by = ax$ giving eigenvector $\begin{bmatrix} b \\ a \end{bmatrix}$

$\lambda = 1-a-b \Rightarrow by = -bx$ giving eigenvector $\begin{bmatrix} 1 \\ -1 \end{bmatrix}$

$\Rightarrow \mathbf{T} = \begin{bmatrix} b & 1 \\ a & -1 \end{bmatrix} \begin{bmatrix} 1 & 0 \\ 0 & 1-a-b \end{bmatrix} \begin{bmatrix} 1 & 1 \\ a & -b \end{bmatrix} \dfrac{1}{a+b}$

$\mathbf{T}^n = \mathbf{U}\mathbf{D}^n\mathbf{U}^{-1}$ where $\mathbf{D}^n = \begin{bmatrix} 1^n & 0 \\ 0 & (1-a-b)^n \end{bmatrix}$

(i)   If $|1 - a - b| < 1$, $\mathbf{D}^n \to \begin{bmatrix} 1 & 0 \\ 0 & 0 \end{bmatrix}$ as $n \to +\infty$

$\Rightarrow \mathbf{T}^n \to \begin{bmatrix} b & 1 \\ a & -1 \end{bmatrix} \begin{bmatrix} 1 & 0 \\ 0 & 0 \end{bmatrix} \begin{bmatrix} 1 & 1 \\ a & -b \end{bmatrix} \dfrac{1}{a+b} = \begin{bmatrix} b & b \\ a & a \end{bmatrix} \dfrac{1}{a+b}$

Thus the subsequent state is independent of the initial conditions in the long term.

(ii)   If $|1 - a - b| = 1$, either $\mathbf{T} = \begin{bmatrix} 1 & 0 \\ 0 & 1 \end{bmatrix}$ and one state or the other permanently

occurs or $\mathbf{T} = \begin{bmatrix} 0 & 1 \\ 1 & 0 \end{bmatrix}$ and the two states alternate.

(continued)

2.   (a)

$$\begin{bmatrix} 3 & 2 & 2 \\ 1 & 4 & 1 \\ -2 & -4 & -1 \end{bmatrix}\begin{bmatrix} 1 \\ 0 \\ -1 \end{bmatrix} = \begin{bmatrix} 1 \\ 0 \\ -1 \end{bmatrix}$$

Eigenvalue 1, eigenvector $\begin{bmatrix} 1 \\ 0 \\ -1 \end{bmatrix}$

$$\begin{bmatrix} 3 & 2 & 2 \\ 1 & 4 & 1 \\ -2 & -4 & -1 \end{bmatrix}\begin{bmatrix} 2 \\ -1 \\ 0 \end{bmatrix} = \begin{bmatrix} 4 \\ -2 \\ 0 \end{bmatrix} = 2\begin{bmatrix} 2 \\ -1 \\ 0 \end{bmatrix}$$

Eigenvalue 2, eigenvector $\begin{bmatrix} 2 \\ -1 \\ 0 \end{bmatrix}$

$$\begin{bmatrix} 3 & 2 & 2 \\ 1 & 4 & 1 \\ -2 & -4 & -1 \end{bmatrix}\begin{bmatrix} 0 \\ 1 \\ -1 \end{bmatrix} = \begin{bmatrix} 0 \\ 3 \\ -3 \end{bmatrix} = 3\begin{bmatrix} 0 \\ 1 \\ -1 \end{bmatrix}$$

Eigenvalue 3, eigenvector $\begin{bmatrix} 0 \\ 1 \\ -1 \end{bmatrix}$

The effect is to stretch by the given eigenvalues along the eigenvectors.

(b)   By multiplication, $UU^{-1} = I$

$$M = \begin{bmatrix} 1 & 2 & 0 \\ 0 & -1 & 1 \\ -1 & 0 & -1 \end{bmatrix}\begin{bmatrix} 1 & 0 & 0 \\ 0 & 2 & 0 \\ 0 & 0 & 3 \end{bmatrix}\begin{bmatrix} -1 & -2 & -2 \\ 1 & 1 & 1 \\ 1 & 2 & 1 \end{bmatrix}$$

$$M^7 = UD^7 U^{-1}$$

$$= \begin{bmatrix} 1 & 2 & 0 \\ 0 & -1 & 1 \\ -1 & 0 & -1 \end{bmatrix}\begin{bmatrix} 1 & 0 & 0 \\ 0 & 128 & 0 \\ 0 & 0 & 2187 \end{bmatrix}\begin{bmatrix} -1 & -2 & -2 \\ 1 & 1 & 1 \\ 1 & 2 & 1 \end{bmatrix}$$

$$= \begin{bmatrix} -1 & 256 & 0 \\ 0 & -128 & 2187 \\ -1 & 0 & -2187 \end{bmatrix}\begin{bmatrix} -1 & -2 & -2 \\ 1 & 1 & 1 \\ 1 & 2 & 1 \end{bmatrix}$$

$$= \begin{bmatrix} 255 & 254 & 254 \\ 2059 & 4246 & 2059 \\ -2186 & -4372 & -2185 \end{bmatrix}$$

(c) $\lambda^3 - 6\lambda^2 + 11\lambda - 6$

$= (\lambda - 1)(\lambda^2 - 5\lambda + 6)$

$= (\lambda - 1)(\lambda - 2)(\lambda - 3)$

Therefore $\lambda = 1, 2$ and 3 satisfy $\lambda^3 - 6\lambda^2 + 11\lambda - 6 = 0$.

$M^3 - 6M^2 + 11M - 6I = 0$

$\Rightarrow M^2 - 6M + 11I - 6M^{-1} = 0$ (multiplying by M^{-1})

$$\Rightarrow 6M^{-1} = M^2 - 6M + 11I$$

$$= \begin{bmatrix} 7 & 6 & 6 \\ 5 & 14 & 5 \\ -8 & -16 & -7 \end{bmatrix} - \begin{bmatrix} 18 & 12 & 12 \\ 6 & 24 & 6 \\ -12 & -24 & -6 \end{bmatrix} + \begin{bmatrix} 11 & 0 & 0 \\ 0 & 11 & 0 \\ 0 & 0 & 11 \end{bmatrix}$$

$$= \begin{bmatrix} 0 & -6 & -6 \\ -1 & 1 & -1 \\ 4 & 8 & 10 \end{bmatrix}$$

$$\Rightarrow M^{-1} = \begin{bmatrix} 0 & -1 & -1 \\ -\dfrac{1}{6} & \dfrac{1}{6} & -\dfrac{1}{6} \\ \dfrac{2}{3} & \dfrac{4}{3} & \dfrac{5}{3} \end{bmatrix}$$

3. (a) Each eigenvalue satisfies the characteristic equation

(b) $a_n M^n + a_{n-1} M^{n-1} + \dots + a_1 M + a_0$

$= a_n (UDU^{-1})^n + a_{n-1} (UDU^{-1})^{n-1} + \dots + a_1 (UDU^{-1}) + a_0$

$= a_n UD^n U^{-1} + a_{n-1} UD^{n-1}U^{-1} + \dots + a_1 UDU^{-1} + a_0 UIU^{-1}$

$= U (a_n D^n + a_{n-1} D^{n-1} + \dots + a_1 D + a_0 I)U^{-1}$

Now $D = \begin{bmatrix} \lambda_1 & & 0 \\ 0 & \lambda_2 & \\ & & \ddots \\ & & & \lambda_n \end{bmatrix}$ and $D^n = \begin{bmatrix} \lambda_1^n & & 0 \\ 0 & \lambda_2^n & \\ & & \ddots \\ & & & \lambda_n^n \end{bmatrix}$

$$\Rightarrow a_n D^n + a_{n-1} D^{n-1} + \dots + a_1 D + a_0$$

$$= \begin{bmatrix} a_n \lambda_1^n & & 0 \\ 0 & a_n \lambda_2^n & \\ & & \ddots \\ & & & a_n \lambda_n^n \end{bmatrix} + \begin{bmatrix} a_{n-1} \lambda_1^{n-1} & & 0 \\ 0 & a_{n-1} \lambda_2^{n-1} & \\ & & \ddots \\ & & & a_{n-1} \lambda_n^{n-1} \end{bmatrix} + \dots$$

$$+ \begin{bmatrix} a_1 \lambda_1 & & 0 \\ 0 & a_1 \lambda_2 & \\ & & \ddots \\ & & & a_1 \lambda_n \end{bmatrix} + \begin{bmatrix} a_0 & & 0 \\ 0 & a_0 & \\ & & \ddots \\ & & & a_0 \end{bmatrix}$$

From (a), the addition of the matrices results in the zero matrix.

Therefore $a_n M^n + a_{n-1} M^{n-1} + \dots + a_1 M + a_0 = 0.$

5 Numerical techniques

5.1 Gaussian elimination

(a) How would you solve these equations?

(b) Describe how you would solve the set of simultaneous equations given above systematically, for example by writing a computer program.

(c) Does your method extend to the solution of 4 x 4 sets?

(d) What is the effect of having rounded data rather than exact integers for the coefficients in the equations? Can you suggest ways of improving the precision?

(a) When applying elimination you probably try to spot 'short-cuts' with the intention of solving the equations as efficiently as possible. In this case, x_3 can be eliminated easily:

$$③ + ①, \qquad 10x_1 + 2x_2 = 12$$

$$② + 2①, \qquad 8x_1 + 5x_2 = 13$$

Then $x_1 = 1$, $x_2 = 1$ and $x_3 = 3$

(b) A computer has to be programmed with a standard method which can be applied in all cases. However, it may be best to give the computer rules designed to make the algorithm as efficient as possible. For example, 'choose the equation with the largest coefficient ...'.

A simple procedure is as follows

- Use equation ① to eliminate x_1 from the other equations.

- Use the new equation ② to eliminate x_2 from the third equation.

The equations are now in the triangular form

$$a_{11}x_1 + a_{12}x_2 + a_{13}x_3 = b_1$$

$$a_{22}x_2 + a_{23}x_3 = b_2$$

$$a_{33}x_3 = b_3$$

- x_3 can be found from the third equation and substituted in the other equations.

- x_2 can be found from the second equation and substituted in the first equation to give the value of x_1.

(c) The procedure of

- using row operations to reduce the equations to triangular form

- using 'back substitution' to solve the equations

generalises to any set of equations. However, problems can arise. For example, the first equation might have a zero coefficient for x_1 or a zero coefficient for one of the variables might occur inconveniently during the process of solution.

(d) Once calculations are made using rounded values, the error inherent in the rounding will grow. There may be many calculations and so rounding can lead to very large errors.

Various methods have been designed to help contain such errors. For instance, it is best to try to avoid fractions, which require rounding if stored in decimal form.

Consider

$$3x_1 + 2x_2 - x_3 = 7 \quad ①$$

$$x_1 + 5x_2 - 3x_3 = 5 \quad ②$$

$$4x_1 - 3x_2 + x_3 = 8 \quad ③$$

Eliminating x_1 would lead to thirds and rounded values. However, if equation ② is put first,

$$x_1 + 5x_2 - 3x_3 = 5 \quad ②$$

$$3x_1 + 2x_2 - x_3 = 7 \quad ①$$

$$4x_1 - 3x_2 + x_3 = 8 \quad ③,$$

eliminating x_1 will produce no fractions.

Numerical procedures work best if you multiply only by numbers smaller than 1 in order to reduce rounding errors.

Temperature distribution

1. It is assumed that constant edge temperatures can be maintained, that the plate is uniform and that there are no losses of heat due to radiation. Problems at the corners of the plate are ignored.

   These are sensible assumptions which may be used to produce a simple first model. More complicated methods would have to be used if the model needed to be refined.

2. (a) $t_1 = \frac{1}{4} (10 + 0 + t_2 + t_4)$

   (b) $t_2 = \frac{1}{4} (t_1 + 0 + t_3 + t_5)$

   $t_3 = \frac{1}{4} (t_2 + 0 + 0 + t_6)$

   $t_4 = \frac{1}{4} (10 + t_1 + t_5 + t_7)$

   $t_5 = \frac{1}{4} (t_4 + t_2 + t_6 + t_8)$

   $t_6 = \frac{1}{4} (t_5 + t_3 + 0 + t_9)$

   $t_7 = \frac{1}{4} (10 + t_4 + t_8 + 5)$

   $t_8 = \frac{1}{4} (t_7 + t_5 + t_9 + 5)$

   $t_9 = \frac{1}{4} (t_8 + t_6 + 0 + 5)$

3. By taking more points a more precise picture of the temperature distribution is obtained.

   The disadvantage is that the number of equations is increased and it is therefore more time consuming to obtain a solution.

1.   (a) $\mathbf{y} = \begin{bmatrix} 2 \\ 4 \\ -3 \end{bmatrix}$

    (b) $\begin{bmatrix} 4 & -2 & 6 \\ 0 & 5 & 1 \\ 0 & 0 & 3 \end{bmatrix} \mathbf{x} = \begin{bmatrix} 2 \\ 4 \\ -3 \end{bmatrix} \Rightarrow \mathbf{x} = \begin{bmatrix} 2.5 \\ 1 \\ -1 \end{bmatrix}$

    (c) $\mathbf{A} = \begin{bmatrix} 1 & 0 & 0 \\ 3 & 1 & 0 \\ 2 & 4 & 1 \end{bmatrix} \begin{bmatrix} 4 & -2 & 6 \\ 0 & 5 & 1 \\ 0 & 0 & 3 \end{bmatrix} = \begin{bmatrix} 4 & -2 & 6 \\ 12 & -1 & 19 \\ 8 & 16 & 19 \end{bmatrix}$

    (d)
$$\begin{aligned} \mathbf{Ux} &= \mathbf{y} \\ \Rightarrow \quad \mathbf{L(Ux)} &= \mathbf{Ly} \\ \Rightarrow \quad \mathbf{(LU)x} &= \mathbf{Ly} \quad \text{(Associativity)} \\ \Rightarrow \quad \mathbf{Ax} &= \mathbf{b} \end{aligned}$$

2.   (a) The first row of **U** simply repeats the first row of the matrix

$$r = 5, \quad s = -3, \quad t = 2.$$

Equating coefficients in the 2nd row of the product:

$$\begin{aligned} rl &= 10 \Rightarrow l = 2 \\ sl + u &= -4 \Rightarrow u = 2 \\ tl + v &= 3 \Rightarrow v = -1 \end{aligned}$$

In the third row

$$\begin{aligned} mr &= 20 \Rightarrow m = 4 \\ ms + nu &= -16 \Rightarrow n = -2 \\ mt + nv + w &= 13 \Rightarrow w = 3 \end{aligned}$$

$$\mathbf{L} = \begin{bmatrix} 1 & 0 & 0 \\ 2 & 1 & 0 \\ 4 & -2 & 1 \end{bmatrix} \quad \mathbf{U} = \begin{bmatrix} 5 & -3 & 2 \\ 0 & 2 & -1 \\ 0 & 0 & 3 \end{bmatrix}$$

    (b) You can use the rows of the product matrix in succession.

(continued)

3.

$$\begin{bmatrix} 2 & -3 & 1 \\ 1 & -1 & 2 \\ 4 & 0 & 1 \end{bmatrix} = \begin{bmatrix} 1 & 0 & 0 \\ \frac{1}{2} & 1 & 0 \\ 2 & 12 & 1 \end{bmatrix} \begin{bmatrix} 2 & -3 & 1 \\ 0 & \frac{1}{2} & \frac{3}{2} \\ 0 & 0 & -19 \end{bmatrix}$$

$$\begin{bmatrix} 1 & 0 & 0 \\ \frac{1}{2} & 1 & 0 \\ 2 & 12 & 1 \end{bmatrix} \mathbf{y} = \begin{bmatrix} 0 \\ -1 \\ 7 \end{bmatrix} \Rightarrow \mathbf{y} = \begin{bmatrix} 0 \\ -1 \\ 19 \end{bmatrix}$$

$$\begin{bmatrix} 2 & -3 & 1 \\ 0 & \frac{1}{2} & \frac{3}{2} \\ 0 & 0 & -19 \end{bmatrix} \mathbf{x} = \begin{bmatrix} 0 \\ -1 \\ 19 \end{bmatrix} \Rightarrow \mathbf{x} = \begin{bmatrix} 2 \\ 1 \\ -1 \end{bmatrix}$$

The solution is $x_1 = 2,\quad x_2 = 1,\quad x_3 = -1.$

Gauss Seidel

1.   (a)

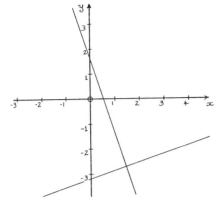

             (b) $x = 1, \quad y = -3$

2.   (a) $x_1 = 1.5, \quad y_1 = -2.67$

            $x_2 = 1.39, \quad y_2 = -2.70$

            $x_3 = 1.40, \quad y_3 = -2.70$

            $x_4 = 1.40, \quad y_4 = -2.70$ (2 decimal places)

            If full calculator accuracy is used :

            $x_4 = 1.399862826$

            $y_4 = -2.700045725$

      (b)   For any starting point, you move horizontally to the first graph and vertically to the second graph.

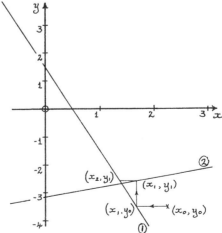

      (c)   For these iterative formulas, the iteration converges for all starting points.

                                                          (continued)

(d)   The method fails for the iteration based on the same pair of equations written in reverse order!

$$2x - 6y = 19 \quad ①$$
$$6x + 2y = 3 \quad ②$$

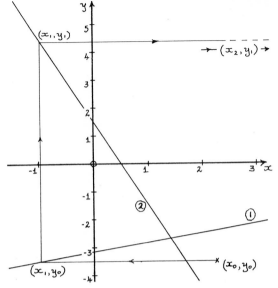

3. $$x_{n+1} = \frac{5 + 3y_n}{8} \quad , \quad y_{n+1} = \frac{11 - 2x_{n+1}}{7}$$

$(x_0, y_0) = (1, 1)$
$(x_1, y_1) = (1, 1.29)$
$(x_2, y_2) = (1.11, 1.26)$ } 2 decimal places
$(x_3, y_3) = (1.10, 1.26)$
$(x_4, y_4) = (1.10, 1.26)$

After 11 iterations the calculations give $x \approx 1.096774194 \quad y \approx 1.258064516$

4.   For $a_{11} x + a_{12} y + a_{13} z = b_1$

$$a_{21} x + a_{22} y + a_{23} z = b_2$$

$$a_{31} x + a_{32} y + a_{33} z = b_3$$

the three iterative equations are

$$x_{n+1} = (b_1 - a_{12} y_n - a_{13} z_n) \div a_{11}$$

$$y_{n+1} = (b_2 - a_{21} x_{n+1} - a_{23} z_n) \div a_{22}$$

$$z_{n+1} = (b_3 - a_{31} x_{n+1} - a_{32} y_{n+1}) \div a_{33}$$

Each new value is calculated using all the most recently calculated values.

Using computer packages

1. (a) $x_1 = 8.08149078 \times 10^{-2}$

   $x_2 = 0.663995365$

   $x_3 = 0.147629622$

   (b) $x_1 = 8.08149078 \times 10^{-2}$

   $x_2 = 0.663995385$

   $x_3 = 0.147629622$

   (c) The residuals are:

(a)	(b)
0	2×10^{-8}
0	3×10^{-7}
0	0

   The initial order appears to be marginally better. This is because the pivots are larger for that order, the multiplying factors are therefore smaller and rounding errors are not magnified as much.

   The difference between orders (a) and (b) might appear insignificant. However, for large arrays the number of errors can build up substantially unless considerable care is taken in setting up the equations for solution.

2. To 2 decimal places, the temperature distribution is:

	0	0	0	
10	4.64	2.37	1.07	0
10	6.20	3.75	1.92	0
10	6.43	4.51	2.86	0
	5	5	5	

3. (a) $x_1 = 8.08149078 \times 10^{-2}$, $x_2 = 0.663995365$, $x_3 = 0.147629622$

   From (0, 1, 0), the solution is accurate to 4 significant figures after 3 iterations.

   (b) The method diverges for all starting values.

4. (a) $x_4 = -0.7907664$, $y_4 = 2.9832376$, $z_4 = 2.95144832$

   (b) $5x_4 - 2y_4 + 4z_4 - 2 = -0.11451392$

   $2x_4 + 8y_4 - 6z_4 - 5 = -0.42432192$

   $x_4 - 2y_4 + 5z_4 - 8 = -3.7 \times 10^{-9}$

Ill conditioning

1. (a) (i) $x = -100$, $y = -149$

    (ii) $x = 100$, $y = 151$.

    There has been a very large change in the solutions despite there having been only a small change in one of the coefficients.

    (b)

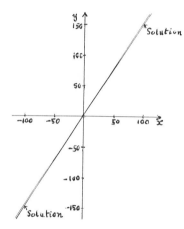

    At this scale it is hard to distinguish the three lines.

    (c) The lines all have very similar gradients so a very small rotation of one line will move the solution a considerable distance.

2. (a) $x = 111$, $y = 10$

    (b) $x = -109$, $y = -10$

    (c)

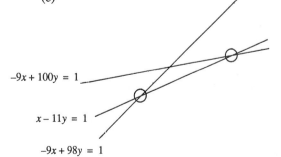

$-9x + 100y = 1$

$x - 11y = 1$

$-9x + 98y = 1$

    The slight change in gradient rotates the line and creates a large change in the solution

    [The scale is distorted to illustrate the effect better.]

3. Any pair of equations such that the gradients of the lines are very similar.

1.   (a)

Operation	y	x	z	c	Row
	1	4	7	9	①
	2	9	−1	11	②
	9	2	−3	5	③
② − 2①	0	1	−15	−7	④
③ − 9①	0	−34	−66	−76	⑤
⑤ + 34④	0	0	−576	−314	⑥

$$x = 1.18, \ y = 0.48, \ z = 0.55 \quad \text{(2 decimal places)}$$

(b)   Rearrange the equations to give a strong diagonal:

$$9x + 2y - z = 11$$

$$2x + 9y - 3z = 5$$

$$4x + y + 7z = 9$$

Then

$$x_{n+1} = (11 - 2y_n + z_n) \div 9$$

$$y_{n+1} = (5 - 2x_{n+1} + 3z_n) \div 9$$

$$z_{n+1} = (9 - 4x_{n+1} - y_{n+1}) \div 7$$

Starting with $x_0 = y_0 = z_0 = 0$, after 6 iterations the values are

$$x_6 = 1.18, \ y_6 = 0.48, \ z_6 = 0.55 \ \text{(2 decimal places)}$$

(c)   Using the same arrangement of the equations as in (a):

$$\begin{bmatrix} 1 & 4 & 7 \\ 2 & 9 & -1 \\ 9 & 2 & -3 \end{bmatrix} = \begin{bmatrix} 1 & 0 & 0 \\ 2 & 1 & 0 \\ 9 & -34 & 1 \end{bmatrix} \begin{bmatrix} 1 & 4 & 7 \\ 0 & 1 & -15 \\ 0 & 0 & -576 \end{bmatrix}$$

Then $\begin{bmatrix} 1 & 0 & 0 \\ 2 & 1 & 0 \\ 9 & -34 & 1 \end{bmatrix} \begin{bmatrix} 9 \\ -7 \\ -314 \end{bmatrix} = \begin{bmatrix} 9 \\ 11 \\ 5 \end{bmatrix}$ and $\begin{bmatrix} 1 & 4 & 7 \\ 0 & 1 & -15 \\ 0 & 0 & -576 \end{bmatrix} \begin{bmatrix} y \\ x \\ z \end{bmatrix} = \begin{bmatrix} 9 \\ -7 \\ -314 \end{bmatrix}$

and the solution is precisely the same as in (a).

(continued)

57

2.   (a)   Gaussian elimination because it is simple and straightforward for small numbers of equations with integer coefficients.

     (b)   Back substitution because the equations are already in an appropriate form.

     (c)   LU decomposition would be best because once **L** and **U** are found only the back substitution would need to be done for each **b**.

3.   (a)   All the methods can be used to find an inverse. The first column of the inverse is

the solution of $\mathbf{Ax} = \begin{bmatrix} 1 \\ 0 \\ 0 \\ \cdot \\ \cdot \\ \cdot \end{bmatrix}$, the second column is the solution of $\mathbf{Ax} = \begin{bmatrix} 0 \\ 1 \\ 0 \\ \cdot \\ \cdot \\ \cdot \end{bmatrix}$ etc.

     (b)   LU decomposition can be used to find $\mathbf{A}^{-1}$ very simply.

$$\mathbf{A} = \mathbf{LU}$$

$$\Rightarrow \quad \mathbf{A}^{-1} = (\mathbf{LU})^{-1}$$

$$\Rightarrow \quad \mathbf{A}^{-1} = \mathbf{U}^{-1}\mathbf{L}^{-1}$$

The inverses of triangular matrices can be found relatively easily.

4.   (a)   (i)   0.67 and 0.63   (2 significant figures)

          (ii)   0.65 and 0.64   (2 significant figures)

     (b) $x = 31,\ y = 20$ (2 significant figures)

     (c) $x = -37,\ y = -24$ (2 significant figures)

     (d) $x \le -37$ or $x \ge 31$ with corresponding values of y.

Note that it is possible for the two lines to be parallel and therefore x lies **outside** the range -37 to 31.

6 Canonical form

6.1 Kernels

(a) Find the general solution of

$$\begin{bmatrix} 2 & 3 \\ 2 & 3 \end{bmatrix}\begin{bmatrix} x \\ y \end{bmatrix} = \begin{bmatrix} 0 \\ 0 \end{bmatrix}.$$

(b) Find a particular solution of

$$\begin{bmatrix} 2 & 3 \\ 2 & 3 \end{bmatrix}\begin{bmatrix} x \\ y \end{bmatrix} = \begin{bmatrix} 5 \\ 5 \end{bmatrix}.$$

(c) Find the general solution of

$$\begin{bmatrix} 2 & 3 \\ 2 & 3 \end{bmatrix}\begin{bmatrix} x \\ y \end{bmatrix} = \begin{bmatrix} 5 \\ 5 \end{bmatrix}.$$

(d) What is the connection between your answers to parts (a), (b) and (c)? Does this result generalise?

(a)
$$\begin{bmatrix} x \\ y \end{bmatrix} = \lambda\begin{bmatrix} -3 \\ 2 \end{bmatrix}$$

(b)
$$\begin{bmatrix} x \\ y \end{bmatrix} = \begin{bmatrix} 1 \\ 1 \end{bmatrix} \quad \text{or} \quad \begin{bmatrix} -2 \\ 3 \end{bmatrix} \quad \text{or} \quad \dots$$

(c)
$$\begin{bmatrix} x \\ y \end{bmatrix} = \begin{bmatrix} 1 \\ 1 \end{bmatrix} + \lambda\begin{bmatrix} -3 \\ 2 \end{bmatrix}$$

(d) A general solution of the equation $\mathbf{Ar} = \mathbf{b}$ appears to be given by a particular solution plus the general solution of the equation $\mathbf{Ar} = \mathbf{0}$.

This is a consequence of the distributive law for matrix algebra:

$$\begin{bmatrix} 2 & 3 \\ 2 & 3 \end{bmatrix}\left(\begin{bmatrix} 1 \\ 1 \end{bmatrix} + \lambda\begin{bmatrix} -3 \\ 2 \end{bmatrix}\right) = \begin{bmatrix} 2 & 3 \\ 2 & 3 \end{bmatrix}\begin{bmatrix} 1 \\ 1 \end{bmatrix} + \lambda\begin{bmatrix} 2 & 3 \\ 2 & 3 \end{bmatrix}\begin{bmatrix} -3 \\ 2 \end{bmatrix}$$

$$= \begin{bmatrix} 5 \\ 5 \end{bmatrix} + \begin{bmatrix} 0 \\ 0 \end{bmatrix}$$

$$= \begin{bmatrix} 5 \\ 5 \end{bmatrix}.$$

Kernels

1. (a)
$$\begin{bmatrix} 1 & 0 & 0 & 1 & 2 \\ 0 & 1 & 0 & -2 & 0 \\ 0 & 0 & 1 & -1 & -1 \\ 0 & 0 & 0 & 0 & 0 \end{bmatrix} \begin{bmatrix} x \\ y \\ z \\ t \\ u \end{bmatrix} = \begin{bmatrix} 0 \\ 0 \\ 0 \\ 0 \\ 0 \end{bmatrix} \Rightarrow \begin{bmatrix} x \\ y \\ z \\ t \\ u \end{bmatrix} = \lambda \begin{bmatrix} -1 \\ 2 \\ 1 \\ 1 \\ 0 \end{bmatrix} + \mu \begin{bmatrix} -2 \\ 0 \\ 1 \\ 0 \\ 1 \end{bmatrix}$$

    (b) The elements in the shaded part of the matrix appear with changed signs in the shaded part of the vectors of the kernel.

2. (a) The conjecture stated in 1(b) will be found to be true for any matrix you have chosen.

    (b) Suppose $\begin{bmatrix} a_1 \\ \vdots \\ a_m \\ \lambda_1 \\ \vdots \\ \lambda_n \end{bmatrix}$ is any vector in the kernel of $\left[\begin{array}{c|c} I & K \\ \hline 0 & 0 \end{array} \right]$

    where I is the $m \times m$ identity matrix and K is an $m \times n$ matrix.

    Then $I \begin{bmatrix} a_1 \\ \vdots \\ a_m \end{bmatrix} + K \begin{bmatrix} \lambda_1 \\ \vdots \\ \lambda_n \end{bmatrix} = 0$

    $$\Rightarrow \begin{bmatrix} a_1 \\ \vdots \\ a_m \end{bmatrix} = -K \begin{bmatrix} \lambda_1 \\ \vdots \\ \lambda_n \end{bmatrix} = -K \begin{bmatrix} \lambda_1 \\ 0 \\ \vdots \\ 0 \end{bmatrix} - K \begin{bmatrix} 0 \\ \lambda_2 \\ \vdots \\ 0 \end{bmatrix} - \ldots$$

    $$= -\lambda_1 k_1 - \lambda_2 k_2 - \ldots \quad \text{where } k_i \text{ is the } i\text{th column of } K.$$

    Then $\begin{bmatrix} a_1 \\ \vdots \\ a_m \\ \lambda_1 \\ \vdots \\ \lambda_n \end{bmatrix} = \lambda_1 \begin{bmatrix} -k_1 \\ 1 \\ 0 \\ \vdots \\ 0 \end{bmatrix} + \lambda_2 \begin{bmatrix} -k_2 \\ 0 \\ 1 \\ \vdots \\ 0 \end{bmatrix} + \ldots + \lambda_n \begin{bmatrix} -k_n \\ 0 \\ 0 \\ \vdots \\ 1 \end{bmatrix}$

Tutorial sheet

1.   (a) $\begin{bmatrix} 1 & -2 & 1 & 1 \\ 3 & -1 & 6 & 1 \\ 1 & 3 & 4 & 3 \end{bmatrix}$

         ②$-3$①, $\begin{bmatrix} 1 & -2 & 1 & 1 \\ 0 & 5 & 3 & -2 \\ 0 & 5 & 3 & 2 \end{bmatrix}$
         ③$-$①,

         $5$①$+2$②, $\begin{bmatrix} 5 & 0 & 11 & 1 \\ 0 & 5 & 3 & -2 \\ 0 & 0 & 0 & 4 \end{bmatrix}$
         ③$-$②,

         $\frac{1}{5}$①, $\begin{bmatrix} 1 & 0 & \frac{11}{5} & \frac{1}{5} \\ 0 & 1 & \frac{3}{5} & -\frac{2}{5} \\ 0 & 0 & 0 & 4 \end{bmatrix}$
         $\frac{1}{5}$②,

         (b)   The 4 in the bottom row shows that the equations are inconsistent and have no solution.

2.   (a) $\begin{bmatrix} 1 & 0 & 0 & -7 \\ 0 & 1 & 0 & -2 \\ 0 & 0 & 1 & 4 \end{bmatrix}$

         (b)   The equations have unique solution $\begin{bmatrix} x \\ y \\ z \end{bmatrix} = \begin{bmatrix} -7 \\ -2 \\ 4 \end{bmatrix}$

3. $\begin{bmatrix} 3 & 5 & 0 & 1 \\ -2 & 1 & 4 & 3 \\ 5 & 17 & 8 & t \end{bmatrix}$ reduces to $\begin{bmatrix} 1 & 0 & \frac{-20}{13} & \frac{-14}{13} \\ 0 & 1 & \frac{12}{13} & \frac{11}{13} \\ 0 & 0 & 0 & t-9 \end{bmatrix}$

         (a) $\lambda \begin{bmatrix} 20 \\ -12 \\ 13 \end{bmatrix}$

         (b)   The equations will be consistent if $t = 9$.

         (c)   When $t = 9$, the general solution is

$$\begin{bmatrix} x \\ y \\ z \end{bmatrix} = \begin{bmatrix} \frac{-14}{13} \\ \frac{11}{13} \\ 0 \end{bmatrix} + \lambda \begin{bmatrix} 20 \\ -12 \\ 13 \end{bmatrix}$$

Programs

The BBC Basic program "GAUSS", given below, enables you to solve N x N simultaneous equations for values of N up to 10. The program uses Gaussian elimination.

```
10      REM PROGRAM GAUSS
20      CLS
30      DIM A(10, 11), X(10)

40      READ N
50      FOR I = 1 TO N
60      FOR J = 1 TO N+1
70      READ A(I, J)
80      NEXT J
90      NEXT I

100     FOR I = 1 TO N-1
110     PIVOT = A(I, I)
120     FOR J = I+1 TO N
130     FACTOR = A(J, I)/PIVOT
140     FOR K = I TO N+1
150     A(J, K) = A(J, K) -A(I, K) *FACTOR
160     NEXT K
170     NEXT J
180     NEXT I

190     FOR I = N TO 1 STEP -1
200     X(I) = A(I, N+1)/A(I, I)
210     FOR J = 1 TO I-1
220     A(J, N+1) = A(J, N+1) - A(J, I)* X(I)
230     NEXT J
240     NEXT I

250     FOR M = 1 TO N
260     PRINT"X";M" = "; X(M)
270     NEXT M

300     DATA 3
310     DATA 50, 1, 2, 5
320     DATA 1, 16, 2, 11
330     DATA 1, 0, 13, 2
```

The coefficients of the equations are read into the matrix A(I, J).

Row operations are used to reduce the matrix to triangular form.

Back substitution is used to solve the equations.

The solutions X1, X2, ... are printed out.

This data is for the 3 x 3 equations:
$$50x_1 + \ x_2 + \ 2x_3 = \ 5$$
$$x_1 + 16x_2 + \ 2x_3 = 11$$
$$x_1 \qquad + 13x_3 = \ 2$$

The use of data lines in "GAUSS" enables you to check if you have input the coefficients correctly and allows you to SAVE the data for particularly large equations. They also make it easy for you to modify the data if you wish to investigate the effect on solutions of rounding errors and of altering the order of the equations.

It is easy to write programs for Gauss Seidel iteration.

For example, the 3 x 3 equations:

$$50x + y + 2z = 5$$
$$x + 16y + 2z = 11$$
$$x + 13z = 2$$

can be solved using Gauss Seidel iteration by programs such as:

fx 7000G

```
?→X: ?→Y: ?→Z
Lbl 1
(5 – Y – 2Z) ÷ 50→X◢
(11 – X – 2Z) ÷ 16→Y◢
(2 – X) ÷ 13→Z◢
"NEXT"
Goto 1
```

BBC BASIC

```
10    INPUT X, Y, Z
20    X = (5 – Y – 2*Z) /50
30    Y = (11 – X – 2*Z) /16
40    Z = (2 – X) /13
50    PRINT X, Y, Z
60    PRINT
70    GOTO 20
```